MW01250474

My Little Grange

To Maritza
From.
Maria Luisa Morel

My Little Grange

✦

The Journey of a Colombian Girl

Maria Luisa Morales

iUniverse, Inc.
New York Lincoln Shanghai

My Little Grange
The Journey of a Colombian Girl

iUniverse books may be ordered through booksellers or by contacting:

iUniverse
2021 Pine Lake Road, Suite 100
Lincoln, NE 68512
www.iuniverse.com
1-800-Authors (1-800-288-4677)

Because of the dynamic nature of the Internet, any Web addresses or links contained in this book may have changed since publication and may no longer be valid.

The views expressed in this work are solely those of the author and do not necessarily reflect the views of the publisher, and the publisher hereby disclaims any responsibility for them.

ISBN: 978-0-595-44280-5 (pbk)
ISBN: 978-0-595-68765-7 (cloth)
ISBN: 978-0-595-88609-8 (ebk)

Printed in the United States of America

Contents

Preface

Even though I have long desired to write a book about my life, it was hard for me to begin—not all my memories are good ones. Once I started writing, though, I had such a sense of relief. My story worked much like therapy for me; I wrote and wrote until my whole life was revealed.

This will be the first time that my family will learn of my childhood—where I came from and what I went through. Putting my experiences in writing felt rather like confessing. I relate here, for the first time, memories that begin when I was about five years old. I wrote the first pages with tears in my eyes—in fact, I cried a lot while writing this book. But every time I wrote a new page, I felt that I was receiving the strength I needed to finish it. My memories of growing up in Colombia during civil conflict are not all bad; I am proud of my Colombian roots, and although I did not have the easiest childhood, I believe that my experiences made me the person I am today. My childhood may not be unique, but it seems so to me.

To this day, Colombia remains involved in a civil war that has been ongoing for as long as I can remember. Colombian guerrilla fighters continue to fight against the government, and many lives are lost each year. It is my hope that one day there will be peace—in the end, it is children who suffer most from the devastating effects of war. People living deep in the countryside still need help; they are struggling to get away from the destruction of the guerillas.

This is the story of my life. Since I moved to the United States in October of 1967, I have returned to Colombia only once to visit my family. Perhaps this book will help my descendents to understand what it was like for me, growing up in Colombia. May God bless all of those who read my story. I am Maria Luisa Morales.

PART I

Childhood Memories of My Family

1

In 1950, I lived in Colombia with my family—my mother, Carlina; my father, Sergio; and my brothers, nine-year-old Avelino and three-year-old Eliecer. I was about five years old. We lived with my grandmother Hermelinda in her big house, as did my aunts Conchita and Trinidad (we called her Trinita) and my uncle Marco. My other uncle, Oliverio, was in the army, but he came home often to visit. Aunt Trinita's son Desiderio lived in the house, too. He was fourteen years old, and I was afraid of him. He would scare Eliecer and me by wearing a mask he'd made from leaves and pumpkin skin, or he would throw sand in our eyes and make us cry.

My grandmother was a hard worker, and she expected my mother and aunts to work hard as well. Often when I woke up in the morning, my mother already was up, helping my aunts milk the cows, feed the chickens, and help with the rest of the domestic animals. Grandma used to make her own thread for sewing, and I was fascinated by the process. First, she would go to the cotton plant, pick the cotton that came from the inside of the dried flower, and make it into a ball. Once she had a good-sized ball, she would grab one strand of the cotton and very carefully roll it onto a top. Then she started the top spinning. She would hold the cotton ball in her left hand while carefully guiding the strand of cotton with her right as the top spun out its growing thread. She called the top *huso*. This process, which she repeated several times, gave us the thread that she would use later to sew our clothes by hand.

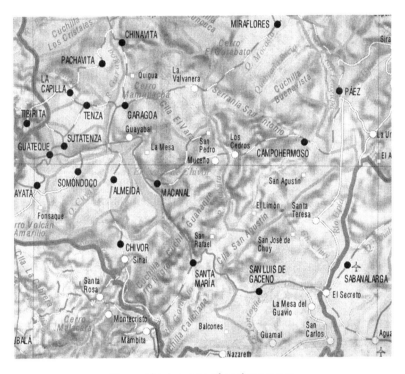

Above: This is a map of my hometown.

My grandmother's property was beautiful, with many fruit trees and a brook. During the day, my brothers and I would go to the brook—even though our mother told us that we shouldn't go by ourselves—and we'd spend the afternoon fishing or catching toads. There was a school in the village, but we didn't go to school: my family didn't seem to care about sending us. We educated ourselves with the many activities we devised to keep us busy.

Grandmother Hermelinda's house was located in the state of Boyaca, about four miles—or half an hour away on horseback—from the small village of Santa Teresa. The village consisted of about eight small houses and a church. No one in Santa Teresa owned a car; horses and donkeys were used for transportation. A larger village, Saint Luis de Gaseno, was about five hours away by horseback and was considered more "civilized" because the people there used cars and buses. If you traveled another five hours by car, you would reach Bogotá, the capital of Colombia.

One of the jobs I was sent out to do was to check if the hens had any eggs. My aunt taught me how to check: I had to stick my little finger under their tails to see if I could feel a hard ball coming from their behinds. If I felt something, then I was to place that hen in a nest and let the other ones free. Sometimes I would help my aunts milk the cows; they used the milk to make butter, desserts, and cheeses.

One day, my aunt Conchita complained at the dinner table that the cat had eaten some cheese and knocked the rest onto the floor. Uncle Marco, who was a hunter and had killed many animals, said, "Don't worry; I'm going to solve this problem." Laughing, he grabbed a thick piece of wood from the yard and went to look for the cat. We all knew he was a hunter but what he was about to do shocked us kids. He brought it back, and in front of all of us children, he laid it on the table with its neck on the thick wood. Then he took out the machete that he carried at his waist and brought it down really hard, cutting off the cat's head, and threw it as far as he could. We stood there in terror for a moment, then began screaming. I started to cry: I had loved that little cat a lot. My aunts also got angry. From then on, I was very afraid of Uncle Marco. Every day, I tried to go see the cat's body, but I couldn't bring myself to out of fear. I was filled with sadness and couldn't forget that awful moment.

My brother Avelino was also a hunter. He made traps to catch quail—not the small bird that's commonly associated with the name quail, but huge black and brown chickens without tails. My aunts used them for making soup. One day, I went to check on Avelino's trap and saw a bird inside of it. Because my brother was not there, and because my aunts always made such a fuss over him when he brought them a quail, I thought that I would bring them the bird—I would be the one they would hug and praise. But the bird was scared, and it clawed and bit me when I took it from the trap. Then it made a horrible noise and started to run away—this type of quail can't fly. I was really scared—partly because the quail bit me, but also because I knew that my brother was going to hit me when he found out what had happened. I entered the house very quietly, hoping not to be noticed. But then I heard Avelino ask, "Who opened my trap?" He knew that it had been me, of course—I couldn't have looked more guilty or scared. Not only did Avelino hit me with a stick, but my aunts were very mad too. And when my grandmother heard the story, she was angriest of all: she sent me to bed without any supper.

I did better collecting the "Ants of May," which arrived every spring. They were huge flying insects, about two inches long and very chubby. They flew in large swarms, and when they landed on the ground they were easy to find because of the bumps they left. We would happily collect these ants—they didn't bite—and my aunts would then place them in a clay pot on the fire to roast. They tasted really good, like popcorn. Some years we saw several swarms of ants, but other years they came only once, and we would have to wait until the following year before we could have our "popcorn."

We also liked to eat guava—that was my favorite fruit. My brothers and I climbed the trees all the time to pick and eat them. The adults told us not to eat too many, or we would get worms in our stomachs. We didn't pay attention to them. Eventually, however, it turned out that the grown-ups were right—my brothers and I ate so much that our stomachs hurt. My aunt sent Desiderio to buy some sort of laxative that would make us have diarrhea.

First, Tia Trinita gave us the medicine. Then, she put a white cloth on the floor and made us push hard on our stomachs. All of a sudden, long, pink tapeworms started coming out. I was horrified to see what had been inside our stomachs. The chickens liked the worms, though, and it was funny to see them pecking at the worms, even as they were still coming out of Eliecer's rear end! We weren't allowed to eat anything until late that night, when we had some chicken broth without salt. After that, we didn't eat guavas again unless my aunts cooked them for marmalade.

Tia Trinita was my favorite aunt because she looked after me. She would comb my long, curly hair, give me a bath, sing with me, and tell me stories that made me laugh. She was very good-looking, too. My other aunt, Conchita, also was pretty but very shy—that may have been because she was a little deaf (we had to shout in order to talk to her). She spent most of her time cooking, washing clothes by the brook, and milking the cows.

On weekends, my mother, my aunts, and my grandmother would make a lot of corn bread, cakes, and *arepas*, corn patties with cheese inside. These goodies weren't for our family, though; my grandmother would bring them to the priest of the local church. Aunt Trinita always asked my grandmother if some goodies could be given to us kids, but Grandma never allowed it. Hermelinda was a very serious woman, who seemed to always be shouting or punishing us: I was afraid of her. So when she said that everything was for the priest, no one questioned it. We were fed yucca, plantains, corn, and lots of pumpkin and fruit; once in a while, Grandma would allow the family to kill a hen to make some soup.

Each Sunday, the adults in my family went to the village of Saint Teresa for mass and to deliver the baked goods to the priest. We children stayed home alone, even though the adults sometimes did not come back home until very late, after we were sleeping. I remember that we cried a lot when we were left alone, especially as it began to get dark outside. We were afraid because we did not have any electricity; all we had for lighting were candles and fireplaces.

When I was five years old, my parents decided to buy a grange—our term for a farm—that was about two hours away from my grandmother's house by horseback. There was a pretty little house on the property, and my parents and my grandmother seemed quite pleased with the idea. The only one who did not share their happiness was my aunt Trinita—she loved me and my brothers so much that she was sad that we would no longer be living together.

Our grange included quite a large piece of property, with many plantain trees, yucca, and pumpkins. The house, which was made of wood with a straw roof, was about eighteen feet square and was one big room. There was also a brook nearby, and after we moved in, we kids spent a lot of time there catching toads and frogs and cooling off on hot days—just as we had at my grandmother's. My dad planted vegetables near the brook: beans, tomatoes, onions. He also bought some chickens and two horses. During harvest time, I used to collect all the vegetables with my dad. I remember how fun it was to collect the multicolored beans, the pumpkins, and the cucumbers. We were kept very busy during this time, but all the vegetables made my mom very happy. Avelino kept catching quail; by this time he had four traps, and we were eating quail almost every day. I had learned my lesson, and I never touched the traps again. We had no neighbors nearby, but we often saw people walking along the road that passed in front of the house. They would wave to us or stop to talk to my mom.

My dad loved my mom—he used to tell people that he had stolen her from her own mother when she was fifteen. Whenever he returned from a trip to the village, he brought her little presents. They seemed to be very happy together.

But our happy family life changed when a man started coming to the house when my dad was not there. My mom liked him because he made her laugh. She would invite him into the house, but she always sent us kids out to get some water or wood, and she asked us not to say anything to Dad about the man's visits. During one of these visits, I came back into the house sooner than she expected, and I saw them together on the bed. They did not see me, but I saw everything that they did. Then I ran out of the house as fast as I could, before my little brother had the chance to follow me and see them.

One morning, when my dad had gone to visit my grandmother, my mom's friend arrived again. On this day he was only in the house for a short time; then he came out and got on his horse, all the while looking at us kids without saying anything. All of a sudden, Mom ran out of the house with a bag in her hands. She got on the horse with that man, and they galloped away. She did not even say good-bye, so we thought that she would be back soon. But as the minutes turned into hours, we started to cry. I knew that nothing would bring her back, but we kept looking at the road, waiting to see if she would return. Finally, much later that night, Dad returned from my grandmother's. Avelino told him that Mom had left with a man on a horse. Dad didn't speak; he just hugged us and started to cry. His sobs were so loud that we kids all cried even harder than before.

Dad hugged us and assured us that Mom would return soon, that we did not need to cry anymore. But days passed, and Mom never came back. Dad went out often—I believe he went to look for her, but of course he never found her. We never saw her again. Ultimately, Dad decided that it was time for us to go back to Grandma's.

I was happy that I would be with Aunt Trinita again, but my enthusiasm might have been somewhat dampened if I'd realized that our journey back to my grandmother's would be so diffi-cult. The sun was very strong on the day we left the grange, and the temperature was almost unbearably hot. We had to stop every few minutes to drink some water or to sit in the shade under the trees. After long hours of traveling, we finally arrived at Grandma's house. Dad hadn't told her what had happened, so she was surprised to see us. When Dad explained, Grandma angrily said that she had never liked Carlina in the first place. Now, she told him, it was time to focus on raising his children. Although Grandma still was quite stern and severe, my aunts were happy that we'd returned; they ran to hug us and to wel-come us. I was happy, too.

Life for my brothers and me was much the same as it had been before we moved to the grange. Grandma kept on baking for the priest, but my aunt Trinita had started answering back to her. My aunt told my grandma not to count on her to help bake any more of those cakes; she wasn't even going to help her bring the goodies to the church. She was very tired of all of that. She stated that she would only bake for those who lived in the house. She also complained that Grandma's only reason for bringing all that food to the church was that she liked hearing the priest complement her from the pulpit. She liked to hear the priest saying that Mrs. Hermelinda Morales was a great person, a generous woman who was always helping the church. My aunt suggested that if my grandmother were truly such a great person, she would not leave her children without any food or goodies. My grandmother used to get mad, but Trinita's words made no difference: she simply took my other aunt, Conchita, with her to deliver her baked goods.

My cousin Desiderio was not happy to have us back in the house: I think he was jealous of the attention we received from his mother. He was always fighting with Avelino, but he seemed to particularly enjoy being cruel to me. He would hit me or tickle me so hard that I would cry. Eventually, he began doing other things to me; he began touching my female parts. When this first happened, I bit his arms so hard that I left marks, but that didn't stop him. I know now that I should have said something to Tia Trinita, but I was afraid of what Desiderio would do if he found out. But because my aunt Trinita had no reason to think that I should not be left alone with him, she sometimes sent me on errands with him. One day, I was told to go with Desiderio to pick ripe coffee, and Desiderio took advantage of the situation. Once we were out in the fields, he threw me to the ground and ripped off all my clothes. I was so afraid that I didn't try to stop him. He forced himself on me for what was to become the first of many instances of sexual abuse. After he'd finished, he whipped me with his belt, threatening to whip me even more if I ever told anyone what he'd done to me. I put on my clothes and followed him, trembling, back to the house. From that point on, my cousin took advantage of me whenever he could. No one in my family suspected anything, and I never spoke of his abuse because I was so afraid of him.

Although Desiderio's abuse was horrifying for me, I soon learned that there were plenty of other things to fear—I heard the grown-ups talking about the guerrillas who had killed people in a faraway village. At the time, I wasn't sure what a "guerrilla" was, but I did understand that they were bad. The members robbed young men and women and then forced them to join their guerrilla forces. This worried everyone very much.

Still, there were happy times, such as when my aunt Trinita became pregnant. Aunt Trinita's boyfriend visited often, almost every day, but toward the end of the pregnancy he disappeared. He was not with her when the time came for her baby to arrive. When she started having labor contractions, only my grandmother and Aunt Conchita were there with her. Desiderio was sent to look for my dad and my uncle Marco. When they arrived, they laid a white sheet on the floor. Trinita lay down on this sheet, and my dad and my uncle each grabbed an end and started to swing her side to side. At the time I didn't know why they did this, but I believe now that it was to help relieve her pain and hasten the delivery. Grandma told us kids to play outside, and later that day Aunt Trinita gave birth to a boy. Once my aunt was relaxed and began to nurse the baby, we all began to think of names. My grandmother said that he would be called José Del Carmen, but my aunt and my uncle Marco did not like this name. Marco suggested Carlos; I said that I wanted him to be named Luis Alberto. I don't know where I had come up with this name, but as soon as I said it my grandmother raised her hand and slapped me hard across the face. She told me to be quiet and let the grown-ups decide. My aunt started to fight with my grandmother, and I began to cry. In the end, my aunt decided on the name my grandmother had chosen, José del Carmen.

Later that day I heard my uncle say that the baby's father had been killed by the guerrilla fighters. He suggested that no one say anything about it to Aunt Trinita—they didn't want to upset her. They wanted her to enjoy her new baby before telling her that José del Carmen's father was dead.

2

My uncle Oliverio came home from the army for a visit. I thought he was nice and funny, and I admired his uniform. Everyone was very happy that he had come home, even though he couldn't stay very long. He told the family to be very careful because of the guerrilla fighting in the other villages.

My dad decided to walk up the mountain to a high point. From there, he could see the village of Saint Teresa, and he knew that if he could see villagers, that would mean there was no danger from guerrillas. But if he didn't see anyone, that meant the villagers were in hiding—and we would have reason to be afraid. He did this each day as a way to keep us safe. One day he came back to the house and told my grandmother that she couldn't go to church—the village looked empty, so they needed to fear the guerrillas.

The guerillas would go from house to house, asking any men they found at home what party they belonged to. If a man guessed wrong, either liberal or conservative, they were shot. If they answered correctly, the guerillas would abduct him and force him to join their party. When my dad, Uncle Marco, Desiderio, and Avelino saw the town empty, they worried and quickly headed for the mountains. My aunts, my grandmother, and we little ones stayed at the house. It was early in the morning, and my aunts continued their daily work. Suddenly, we saw six men approaching very quickly on horseback; they were armed with shotguns and rifles. They rode up to the house, dismounted quickly, and pushed their way inside.

"Where are the men?" one of them shouted at Trinita.

Tia Trinita froze in fear, but Grandma spoke up bravely. "There are no men here," she said. "What do you want?"

One of the men pointed his rifle out the door, toward the chickens. "Kill some of those and cook up some yucca and plantains too. And be quick about it!"

My aunts and grandmother started to do as they were told, but one of the men held out his rifle to block their way. "Which political party do you belong to," he growled, "liberal or conservative?"

"I don't understand," Grandma said convincingly. She knew if she said the wrong thing, we could all be killed right there. "I don't know what those parties are. We don't belong to any party."

Without any hesitation, the men grabbed Aunt Trinita and threw her into a room.

"Please!" Grandma yelled. "Don't touch her! She's just had a baby!"

The men either didn't hear her or chose to ignore her, because then they grabbed Aunt Conchita and threw her into the same room. I watched, horrified, as the men undressed my aunts, threw them on the floor, and began to abuse them. Grandma had the baby in her arms, but she gave him to me, and I also held onto my brother Eliecer. We sat very quietly on the floor near my grandmother.

One of the men came out of the room and held a gun to Grandma. "Cook! Quickly!" he demanded.

Grandma did her best, but we could hear my aunts screaming, and my grandmother got more and more nervous. When she finished cooking, those savages ate like animals, and then, just as suddenly as they'd arrived, they disappeared.

Then there was a great silence. Grandma ran to check on my aunts. "Go outside with the children," she called to me over her shoulder. I gathered up Eliecer and baby José and quickly went out the door. We stood in the yard, waiting, and still there was absolute silence. About an hour later, Grandma came out and hugged me very tightly—this surprised me because she had never hugged me—but she didn't say a word. I could tell she was weeping. She seemed afraid, and so were we. The next morning, Avelino returned to the house alone.

"Where is your father?" she asked. "Where are Marco and Desiderio?"

"They sent me ahead," Avelino answered, "to find out if you've seen anything."

Grandma nodded her head sadly. "Yes, Avelino. Tell your father not to come back here. The guerrilla fighters were here just yesterday, and they questioned us. It is not safe."

Avelino turned and ran toward the mountains again, but instead of following Grandma's advice, he returned shortly after that with my father, Uncle Marco, and Desiderio. "We've only come back for supplies," my father explained. "We'll need some fruit and drinks. And I'm taking Maria and Eliecer with Avelino and me now." My father explained to the women that it would be best if we all left the house and went in different directions to the next town. My brothers and I joined my father and headed back toward the mountains, but Uncle Marco and Desiderio went in a different direction. We walked until my father decided we could stop for a rest under some large trees. I was so mentally and physically tired that I fell down like a rock and was soon asleep.

At sunrise my father woke us, and we continued walking. Eliecer complained that his feet hurt—mine did, too, because we were barefoot and had to climb over boulders and a lot of smaller rocks—but we had to keep going. We saw many different animals on that journey—snakes, iguanas, birds, and monkeys. My dad was in the lead, but he sometimes had to carry Eliecer, who was crying. When the sun was high, we rested for a while and ate the last of the fruit that we had brought. Then we continued walking; it was already late in the day, and Dad had decided that we needed to make our way off of the mountain to see if we could find someone who could give us some information about the guerrilla fighters.

And so we walked and walked until we came down from the mountain and could see a little house off in the distance. We headed toward it, but with great caution—we had to stay constantly alert for anyone on horseback, because the guerrilla fighters rode horses. When we'd almost reached it, Dad told us to wait under a tree while he went up to the house. After he walked away, though, we three kids ignored his words. We scurried across the field and went behind the house to look for food or something to drink. As we walked to the back of the house, I saw a large hole in the ground, large enough to fit two bodies. All I remember seeing was four legs sticking straight up out of that ditch—they looked like posts—and two headless bodies nearby. Flies were swarming everywhere.

We ran around the side of the house to find Dad, who quickly stopped us from going any further. He told us not to go to the front of the house, because there was a dead dog there. We brought him to the back of house and showed him the bodies. He looked extremely afraid. He took off his hat and bowed, saying a quick prayer, but then we all ran back toward the mountains again. I experienced a moment of horror when I felt someone pull at my hair, but then I realized it was just caught in the branches of a tree. I was so frightened by what we had just seen that I didn't notice the pain in my legs and feet any-more—I just kept running. Dad had to carry Eliecer, and Avelino seemed very tired. We came to a brook and were able to drink water, and my dad filled up his canteen. We hadn't eaten since we'd finished the fruit several hours earlier, and as our ter-ror diminished, we felt more and more tired.

As the sun started setting and the forest got dark, Dad decided that we would stop to sleep. Again, I fell asleep almost immediately, nestled under a tree. I awoke early the next morn-ing to the song of birds and the sounds of other animals. Dad gave each of us some water to drink, and then he cuddled us and told us jokes, but none of us laughed now. It was time to continue our journey, so although we were very hungry, we started walking again. Fortunately, we soon saw a grange with a lot of fruit trees. We approached it very cautiously and picked some guavas. Even though I could still remember the experience with the tapeworms, I didn't care—I was too hungry not to eat the fruit. We picked a lot of them to take with us—and thank God, no one saw us. The only other creatures around were cat-tle and horses.

Later that day, after we'd covered a great distance, Dad said he was somewhat oriented as to where we were. "We're going to head to a town called Santa Maria," he said, "but I think it will be better if we sleep in the mountains again."

After drinking water and eating more guavas, we went to sleep; it wasn't dark yet, but we were very tired.

The next morning, we began our trek once again. Eliecer was able to walk on his own now, and that made it somewhat easier for us to move. We had walked for a few hours when Dad suddenly shouted, "Stop! A poisonous snake!" He grabbed a long, dry stick and whacked the snake on its head until he'd killed it. Then he tossed down the stick and guided us around its still-venomous body. "Walk carefully," he warned. "Snakes don't travel alone, so its partner is probably nearby."

"What if we see it?" Avelino asked.

"Don't worry," Dad said reassuringly. "We can take care of that one, too. Just remember that snakes have to be killed by hitting them on the head, and you have to use a very long, thin stick. The stick also has to be dry—not green—or the snake's venom will travel through the stick and onto your hands, and that will kill you."

We walked in silence for a while, watching for snakes as well as for signs that there might be guerrilla forces nearby.

Finally, Dad stopped and wiped his arm across his forehead, mopping the sweat from his brow. "That house up ahead seems familiar to me," he said. "At least … I think it is." He turned and gave us a stern look. "I want you children to wait here. Don't follow me this time."

He ran to the house, and we waited as we'd been told. A man and a woman came out of the house and spoke with Dad; then he signaled us to join them. As we approached, he was telling the people about the bodies we'd discovered at the first house.

"We knew that there were guerilla forces in the area," the man said. "But we didn't know about the killing."

"It's horrifying," the woman agreed, "but I don't think our place is dangerous. We're near a town, and there are police to protect us. Guerillas aren't going to come here."

We stayed with the couple for the rest of the night. We slept on the floor, but we didn't mind that—we knew that we were safer with them than sleeping under the trees.

The next day we left very early for Santa Maria. We walked for hours and hours—nearly the entire day—and when we arrived in the town, I was surprised to find Grandma, my aunts, and baby José already there. They took one look at us and said things like, "Oh, poor things!" and "Look at those feet!" Dad told them everything about our journey, including the dead couple we'd seen.

"Thank God you made it here alive!" Grandma cried.

My aunts took Eliecer and me down to a small river and bathed us. By the time we returned to where Grandma was staying, Dad and Avelino had disappeared: because of the guerilla warfare, my family decided it was best for the men to go their separate ways. I never saw my dad, my brother Avelino, or my uncle Marco again.

That night Eliecer and I stayed with my aunts at their friends' house. I cried about Avelino, especially, because I loved him a lot, and I didn't know what had become of him. "He'll be back soon," Tia Trinita said soothingly. "Don't worry, Maria. He'll be fine."

3

A few days later, Grandma and my aunts decided it would be best for us to go to Garagoa, a large town that was a few hours away from Santa Maria. They were excited about the move; in Garagoa, they thought, they would find work and be able to support us all. Our route to Garagoa took us not through the mountains but along a busy road. I had never in my life seen a truck or a bus; I had only heard my aunts and other people talk about them. These vehicles passing alongside us seemed like something from another world to me.

We walked for almost half a day, passing others who were fleeing the guerrillas. Our fellow travelers had terrible stories—how they were killing innocent people, how they were kidnapping girls, and how they were forcing people like us to leave behind their granges, houses, and animals to avoid losing their lives.

After we had walked for some time, we stopped to rest along the side of the road. We were sitting on some rocks, watching the traffic, when a truck pulled to a stop next to us. A man got out and spoke with my aunt Trinita, then she called out to us, sounding quite happy—the man had offered us a ride. He helped us to climb onto the bed of his truck, which had a fence around the sides. We were all very content, but when the truck started moving, I became quite nervous. I squeezed Aunt Trinita's hand very tightly and started crying, but she gradually calmed me down, and I wasn't so afraid.

When we arrived at Garagoa, the man told Aunt Trinita that he had a garage and that we could stay there. Because we didn't know anyone and had nowhere to go, Aunt Trinita gratefully accepted his offer. The man brought us to our new lodgings, which didn't have a door but did have a roof, and told us about a local priest who was helping others on the run from the guerillas. "Maybe he can help you, too," he said, before telling us good-bye and leaving us for the night.

"I can't believe what a good man he is," Aunt Conchita said.

"Thank God we met him," Aunt Trinita agreed.

That night, we stayed in the garage; it became our new home, at least for the time being. We didn't have any food, but there was a little river nearby where we could get water. The floor of the garage was made of concrete, and it had a lot of gaps. The garage itself had another unit attached to it where some men were living—we knew that because we could hear them talking at night. My aunts liked the fact that there were no houses near the garage; that meant that there was a lot of land we could use to go to the bathroom. In the morning, Aunt Trinita and Grandma went to the church, which was about three blocks away, so they could talk with the priest. They hoped that he could help us, because we had nothing to eat. When they came back a little later, they had bread and a lot of grains to make soup, as well as clothes for the baby and Eliecer.

Little by little, we went out more to get to know the town. It seemed like a very noisy town to me—there were a lot of people talking, horses neighing, mules braying, and the noise of many carts. My aunts and my grandmother fashioned beds for us by putting rocks on the floor, covering them with sticks, and top-ping the arrangement off with wooden planks and little blankets that the priest had given us. People gradually gave us pots and other things that we needed to cook, and my aunts used three large rocks to fashion a fire pit where they could cook corn soups and other simple dishes.

By the time we'd been there for a month, however, my aunts still hadn't found any work, and my grandmother was becoming more and more unbearable. She would hit me and Eliecer for no reason. She'd make us cry by insulting us and telling us that she didn't want us near her. And she fought with Aunt Trinita because she wanted to move to a better place.

But soon Tia Trinita began washing clothing for other people. She went very early in the morning to the river, where she washed the clothes, and she didn't return until very late. I missed her a lot, and because my grandmother didn't cook for us, we spent our days feeling very hungry. Tia Conchita never found work but she was very helpful at home, taking care of the kids and helping to cook.

One Sunday, Tia Trinita decided to take me to church. I didn't have any dresses to wear except a long white dress that Grandma had made a long time ago. After the mass, Tia Trinita and I went to the vestry to see the priest.

"What is your name, child?" he asked.

"Maria Luisa Morales," I answered.

"What a pretty name, little girl," he said, laughing. Then he patted my shoulder. "I have some dresses that I think you would find useful."

I was happy to hear this, and even happier when I saw the dresses—some were dark blue and some were white; they were below the knee with puffy short sleeves, and they had ruffles on the collar and the skirt. They all seemed incredibly beautiful to me; I had never seen dresses like these—to wear such dresses was like a dream for me. Grateful and excited, we thanked the priest, and he gave us some more food to bring home.

When we got home—for that is how I thought of our garage by this time—I very happily showed Grandma my dresses. I started to put one on so she could see how I looked in it, but she scowled at me and said, "That dress is too short! Don't even think that I'm about to let you wear it!" With that, she took the dresses from me, saying she would "fix them" the next day. But I was just a little girl, and I wanted to wear one of the dresses. Crying, I begged her to let me wear it. This just made her angrier. Aunt Trinita tried to speak for me, but that just led to another argument between her and Grandma. Aunt Conchita never got involved in the problems between Trinita and Grandma. She was very quiet and calm, but I always thought that was mostly because she didn't hear my grandmother's shouting.

The next day, I woke Grandma very early so that she could fix my dress; after a while, she went out to buy what she needed to fix it. When she returned, she had a piece of red fabric. She took one of the dresses and cut it at the waist, sewed on a huge piece of the red fabric—it was about ten inches wide—and reattached the skirt. When I saw my pretty white dress with the red fabric in the middle, I started crying. And when Grandma saw my reaction to her work, she slapped me hard across my face. My nose started bleeding, but this time Aunt Trinita wasn't there to defend me. Grandma then calmly took the other dress and did the same thing. Both dresses now looked awful to me, but she forced me to wear one. "See how pretty it looks on you?" she said. "That is how you should dress—so that the skirt almost reaches the floor." She took my old white tunic and hid it, saying that I now had two beautiful dresses to wear.

When Aunt Trinita returned, I was still very sad about the dresses, and she noticed right away. "What's wrong, Maria?" she asked.

I just shook my head. I didn't want to say anything, because I was afraid of making Grandma angry again, but Aunt Trinita realized what the problem was as soon as she saw the dresses. She had another fight with Grandma because of it, but the damage had already been done.

Later, she told us that she had good news—she had found a little house, about fifteen minutes away. It had two rooms and a little kitchen. We would have to pay rent, but the amount was small. Since she was working, she could pay it. My grandmother was happy, and so were we. A few days later, we moved into our pretty little house. The previous renters had left a bird named Roberto, who talked at all hours. I loved that bird, and he became my great friend. I took him everywhere on my shoulder. I fed him pumpkin seeds, fruit, and pieces of bread—when we had it. Our house overlooked a fairly busy path, and when Roberto saw people coming, he would say, "Adios, putas," *Goodbye, bitches*. The first time we heard him say this, we got a little scared. Grandma said that his former owners had probably left him behind because he was so crude. Eventually, though, we taught him to say "frutas," *fruit,* instead of "putas."

We hadn't been in the house very long when Grandma got sick. She said that her head and stomach hurt a lot, although she never went to a doctor. Because she was ill, though, I was the one who did the chores. When I needed to go into town to get something we needed, I had to wear one of those dresses—I didn't have anything else. Sometimes girls would laugh at me, and I got really embarrassed.

People continued to arrive in Garagoa as they fled from the guerrillas. The result was that the priest could not continue to help us by giving us food, because there wasn't enough for everyone. We grew very hungry, because Aunt Trinita didn't earn enough money to buy food. Then Aunt Conchita suddenly became sick; she cringed with stomach pains. Grandma gave her herbal waters and other household remedies for the pain, but Conchita only got worse, and after a while, I saw blood on her skirt. Grandma took her to the river, and when they returned much later, I heard Grandma tell Aunt Trinita that she was happy Conchita had lost the baby—that it was the best thing that could have happened. I didn't understand why Grandma would say such a thing; at my young age, I didn't realize that Aunt Conchita's baby was a result of her being raped by the guerrilla fighters.

Because we were often hungry, I made it my job to find sweet potatoes. I looked for the leaves I had learned to recognize, then dug until I found them. Then I would bring them to my grandmother or Aunt Conchita so that they could cook them—this made them both very happy. Our meals each day consisted of soups with flour and sweet potatoes; there wasn't much, but it satisfied our hunger. I ate everything down to and including the skin. One day, my grandma sent me to buy a small pound cake, but on the way home I was so hungry that little by little I ended up eating almost half of the cake. When my grandmother saw what I'd done, she took a stick and hit me so hard that she left marks on my legs. When my aunt Trinita found out, she was so angry that my grandmother had scolded me for eating the cake; she felt that my grandmother was selfish and wrong in helping the priest in the old town and not helping her own family. She angrily asked my grandmother where that priest is now, "now that we are in so much need." She also told my grandmother that she was selfish and didn't love her grandchildren.

My grandma kept feeling sick, and sometimes she couldn't even get up. I continued to do the chores. Suddenly, though, she seemed to get better and began to go out with a friend she had met when we lived in the garage. One day, the friend came to our little house, and she and Grandma cooked and barbecued meat. I could smell the delicious aroma all day and could hardly wait until it was time to eat. But Eliecer and I were sent to fetch water, and when we returned all that was left was the usual corn soup.

The next day Grandma hugged me and said she was taking me to town with her to buy a few things. I was really happy, because Grandma was never so kind to me. The change in her seemed like a dream to me. When we got to town, she took me to a very pretty house. We knocked on the door, and my grandmother's friend came out. She invited us in and told us to follow her to the kitchen—she was the cook. She left us in the kitchen while she went to look for the owner of the house, then pointed to me and said, very loudly, "This is the girl we talked about."

What was happening? I didn't understand.

The owner of the house looked down at me. "You will be helping to take care of my children," she said. "You'll also help Matilde by doing whatever she tells you." She smiled thinly, then turned to my grandmother's friend and said pointedly, "Give her a good bath."

Matilde grabbed me by the arm and ushered me out of the kitchen. I looked back for my grandmother, but she was already gone. Everything had happened so fast, I couldn't believe what was happening to me. Matilde bathed me and put new clothes on me, but I only wanted to go back to my family. I didn't have any idea where I was, because I hadn't been paying attention when Grandma had brought me to this house. All I knew was that my home was far away and that I already missed my little brother.

I tried to leave later that afternoon, but Matilde was watching me and I couldn't get away. She was actually very kind, and treated me nicely, so it wasn't all bad. Later, the woman's husband and two children came home. The children were beautiful; one was about four years old, and the other was about two. Matilde continued to watch me, but now she told me that if I were to try to leave, the man or the woman would call the police and have me taken away to a very dark place—where they ate people! I believed what she told me; I had no reason to think she would lie to me.

That night, I slept in Matilde's room, which was very pretty and very clean, but I felt an unending sadness. I didn't know if I would ever see my family again. I couldn't sleep because I was thinking about my older brother, Avelino. I missed him, too, and didn't know anything about how he was. Oddly enough, I didn't really miss my mom and my dad anymore—and of course, I hated my cousin Desiderio and hoped I would never see him again. But I thought of Avelino and Eliecer and about my aunt Trinita a lot—I wondered if she knew that Grandma had brought me to this place.

When I had been at the woman's house for about three days, she saw a scratch on my leg that she said looked infected.

"How did you get this scratch?" she asked.

"When we were walking through the mountains," I answered.

"Matilde," the woman ordered, "put cream on that scratch right away. I don't want her to have anything that's contagious."

When the husband came home and learned about the situation, he was afraid for his children. "We need to return this girl," he insisted. "I don't want her here."

The woman quickly gave me some coins and some clothes, then she turned to Matilde: "Take her back where she came come from."

I was so happy that I hugged Matilde and gave her a kiss on the cheek. We walked together until I finally saw scenery I recognized. I was by the river where my aunt Trinita washed clothes.

"I know this place," I told Matilde. "I can go on my own from here."

Matilde smiled at me. "Good-bye, Maria."

4

Although I was glad to be back home, I felt afraid when I remembered Grandma's happiness when we'd gone to the woman's house. Now I knew that she'd been happy because she was giving me away. As I continued walking, I wondered if Aunt Trinita had agreed to the plan; I was very confused. Then I saw Aunt Trinita, doing her washing with a few other women. I sat down right there and waited for her to see me. When she did, she dropped everything in her hands and ran over to me, crying. I also started to cry as I hugged her.

"Where have you been all this time?" she sobbed. "I looked everywhere for you! I was so angry with your grandmother for leaving you alone in the store!"

"I don't know," I said quietly. "A woman brought me to her house and wouldn't let me leave." I was afraid to tell Tia Trinita that Grandma had given me away.

I waited patiently while Tia Trinita finished washing, and then we returned to our little house. I was very happy because I knew that my aunt hadn't wanted to give me away. When we walked into the house, Eliecer ran out to hug me. So did Aunt Conchita. Grandma, though, was sick in bed. Later, Aunt Trinita told Grandma that she had found me and that I was safely home.

"Hello, Grandma," I said quietly, although I didn't step very close to her.

"It's good that you're back, Maria," she said, but her voice was cold. "I need you to do the chores—you know that Aunt Conchita isn't very good at them."

"Yes, Grandma, whatever you say."

Soon after that, my uncle Oliverio came to visit us. He brought us food, clothes, and money.

"God has brought you from heaven, Oliverio!" Grandma said. "We have been in need!"

"I didn't come only to bring things for you, Mama," he said. "I have news." He lowered his voice then, as if afraid someone might overhear. "You can't return to our town. There are still a lot of guerrilla fighters killing people. Our army is there, though, and it has been confronting the guerrillas. Soon, maybe, I will have better news."

Before he left, he took Grandma to a doctor. He gave her some medicine, but he also told her that she had to stop eating foods with sugar: her blood sugar was very high, and this was dangerous.

Aunt Trinita continued washing clothes. I always liked to go with her, because I didn't want to stay with my grandma—I was afraid that she would give me away again. By this time, though, Grandma was getting sicker and sicker. She frequently suffered from diarrhea, but she was too weak to get out of bed, so she had to use a chamber pot. After she used it, she would call me to take it outside and bury it in a hole. If I didn't come quickly, she would hit me with the stick that she kept at her side. Sometimes, when I returned the chamber pot, I left it far from her bed because I was afraid go closer.

I continued trying to find sweet potatoes, because I liked them a lot and they satisfied my hunger. But there were hardly any left now. Those that I did find were often tiny and green.

Sometimes I didn't hear Grandma calling for me because I was out looking for potatoes. When I returned, she would call me again and sweetly say, "Come here, my little child. Take this." When I got close to her, she would take out the stick and hit me very hard, saying, "That is so that you will come quickly when I call."

Grandma's health was not improving, and my aunts were quite worried. Finally, Grandma told Aunt Trinita to call for the priest: she wanted to make her last confession. Trinita ran to get him, but by the time he arrived, Grandma had become very quiet. We were all very sad because she looked so pale and exhausted. The priest gave the services, and that night, my grandma died. Conchita and Trinita shut Eliecer and me in a room right away so that we wouldn't see my grandma's dead body, and some men came and carried her away in a box. We all cried uncontrollably. It had seemed like Grandma would always be with us: I had never thought about her dying. Even though she hit me and never showed any love for me, I still missed her.

About a month after Grandma died, Aunt Trinita told me that she had learned of a school for girls. "It would be very good for you to go to school," she encouraged me. "You'd learn a lot, because you're very smart." She stroked my hair and smiled at me. "I'm going to take you there tomorrow."

I felt the same emptiness in my stomach I had when Grandma had given me away, and I started to cry. "I don't want to go alone! Please, Tia Trinita! Don't make me go!"

"It's for your own good, Maria Luisa," she insisted. "Some day, you'll thank me for making sure you got an education."

PART II

Life at the Infant Grange of Father Luna

5

The next morning, Aunt Trinita collected my things in a bag. She told Aunt Conchita and Eliecer that I was going to a very nice school to study and that I was going to do very well. "We'll visit Maria often," she said, "but now it's time for us to leave."

We went into town, and Aunt Trinita asked a man with a truck for a favor. "Could you take us to Tenza?" I wasn't happy as we climbed onto the truck, but my aunt hugged me and tried to comfort me. "It won't be forever, Maria," she assured me. "And we'll come to visit you. I promise."

Tenza was a very big town, with a lot of people in the streets and many tables at the market where food was sold. Music filled the air, and there were lots of stores. We continued through the town to the outskirts, until we came to a sign on a building that read "Infant Grange of Father Luna."

"This is your stop," the man said to Trinita. "Wait for me here, and I'll come back for you in half an hour."

We thanked him, climbed off the truck, and entered the building. There, Aunt Trinita spoke with two women.

"The priest of Garagoa tells me that you take children whose parents are very poor or who are orphans," Trinita began, hopefully.

"Yes, we do," one of the women said, "but this place is only for boys. There's another school that takes in girls, but it's very far away, past Bogotá."

Aunt Trinita looked distraught. "Please take her," she begged. "I can't take her any farther because I have two other smaller children at home, and I can't leave them alone any longer. Maria is my little niece—her parents left her with me, but I can't support her or send her to school."

The other woman was shaking her head. "I'm afraid we can't—"

"We've been living in Garagoa," Trinita went on. "We came there from a little town called Santa Teresa, which we had to leave because of the guerrillas. They're still killing people—I don't know if we'll ever be able to go back."

"We've heard about that," the woman replied. "I'm very sorry for your troubles." She looked at her companion then, and the two of them seemed to come to a silent agreement. The woman nodded. "All right. You may leave the child with us. When our general director, Señorita Anita returns, we'll take Maria to the Infant Grange for girls."

My aunt was very happy and said good-bye to me. I cried, as always, but the women did their best to soothe me. It wasn't until much later that they realized they'd forgotten to ask for my information—they hadn't even asked Trinita for her name.

I told them that my name was Maria Luisa Morales and that my aunt was named Trinidad Morales.

"Very good, Maria Luisa." The woman smiled at me. "My name is Maria, too—I am Señora Maria."

"And I am Señorita Rita," the other woman said. "Do you know your date of birth?"

I shrugged; I had never heard of this before.

They looked at each other and laughed, and Señora Maria said, "Don't worry about it—we'll find out. You look like you must be about seven years old."

They took me to the kitchen and gave me something to eat. They bathed me, lamenting the ragged clothes I'd come in and the fact that I'd arrived barefoot. Señorita Rita took out a piece of paper and asked me to step on it. She traced my foot with a pencil and then left for a while. Señora Maria wrapped me in a towel and brought me to a room.

"Wait here," Señora Maria said. "We're going to buy you some clothes."

Although I was being treated well, I was very sad because it seemed that little by little, I was leaving my family behind. First my mom, then my dad, my older brother Avelino, and my uncle Marco. Then my grandma had died, and I had now lost my aunt Conchita, my little brother Eliecer, the baby, and my aunt Trinita. I wasn't mad at my aunt Trinita, since she'd explained everything to me before bringing me here, but I couldn't help feeling frightened and sad.

After a while, Señora Maria returned with a bag of clothes and some white shoes. No one had ever bought shoes for me! And the clothes were so pretty.

"What do you think, Maria Luisa?" Señora Maria asked as she helped me to dress. "Do you like these clothes?"

"Oh yes, I do! Thank you very much!" For a while, I forgot my sadness and enjoyed my new clothes and shoes.

Then I heard children's voices outside and rushed to the window. There were about fifty of them, all in a line. Señora Maria told me they had just gotten out of their classes. I soon learned that there were many teachers here; there also were cooks and people who cleaned. Señorita Rita was the school's director, and Señora Maria was her assistant. They didn't leave me alone, not even for one moment, and they often called to me to come stay with them. The food they served at the school was delicious, and there was such abundance that for the first time in a long time, I was able to eat until I was no longer hungry.

Señorita Rita told the teachers that I was going to stay with them until Señorita Anita could take me to the Infant Grange for girls. All the teachers seemed to like to pet my head; they were very kind to me. Señora Maria liked to brush my hair, braiding it with ribbons so long that they reached my waist. Señorita Rita put a cream on the scratch on my leg, even though she told me it was already healed. She asked me how I had scratched it, and I told her about our journey through the mountains. She seemed very frightened for me and said, "Oh, poor little thing."

About two weeks later, Señorita Anita came to the grange. She was a very tall woman with short hair and creamy white skin. She spoke precisely and was very elegant. Everyone rushed to greet her, and Señorita Rita told her about my situation. I was afraid and began to cry for the first time since I'd arrived, but she hugged me and told me not to worry, that she was going to bring me to a place with a lot of girls and that I was going to be fine. Little by little, she began to win my trust. Then she told Señorita Rita to bring the scissors so that she could cut my hair. I loved my hair—it had never been cut—but I was afraid to say anything. Señorita Anita cut it very short, but she loved cutting it. I never understood why she cut my hair, she never gave me an explanation.

Señorita Anita and I left for the capital city the next morning. Bogotá was three or four hours away by car, and I got so carsick and dizzy that the driver had to stop to let me rest for a while. Señorita Anita eventually gave me something to eat and a lemon to sniff during the trip, which helped enough with the car sickness that I was able to fall asleep. It was nighttime when I woke up, and we were in Bogotá.

I woke to people and lights everywhere, and lots of cars. It was unlike anything I had ever known. Señorita Anita brought me to a big house with many people: this was where I was to stay until I could go to the Infant Grange for girls. The workers there treated me very well. I spent my time at the window, watching the cars, the people, the other children, and all the other sights outside.

Señorita Anita came back two days later and happily told me, "Maria Luisa, we are heading to the girls' grange, which is going to be your home." I was very happy that I would be with other girls, but I was also thinking about my family. They did not know anything about what was happening to me or where I was going. Everything seemed to be so complicated, and I seemed to be moving farther and farther away from them.

We traveled for about two hours before we reached a little village called Alban. I didn't know why we were stopping in the village, but I soon found out—I was to receive my first shots. I thought the shots were painful, but Señorita Anita told me that they were necessary to help me stay healthy. Our journey continued for about another hour after that, and then we reached the Infant Grange of Father Luna. When we arrived, all the girls stood in a line to greet Señorita Anita and to sing some songs. I loved it, but I was feeling a little shy. I hid behind Señorita Anita until she handed me over to a nun named Mother Maria Luisa—her name was just like mine! She hugged me and called me her "buddy," because we both had the same name. Once the girls finished with their songs, Mother Maria Luisa clapped her hands and announced, "Girls, I am going to introduce you to your new little sister. I would like you to take care of her, because she is very small and in great need of love."

The girls started asking questions, wanting to know my name and where I'd come from, but I was very shy and didn't say much. There were many girls—maybe fifty of them, of all different ages—and they all were wearing the same type of beige dress with a belt. They looked very pretty and smart.

When the girls went to lunch, a nun named Mother Rosario guided me inside the building. She took my clothes and placed them in a box, which had the number thirty-four on it. "This will be your box, Maria," she explained. "Put everything you have in here." Then she gave me some uniforms, telling me to try them on and keep the one that fit best. When I was dressed in my uniform, Mother Rosario took me back to Señorita Anita. "Doesn't she look nice, Señorita?" Mother Rosario asked.

Señorita Anita smiled at me and nodded, then directed her attention to the nun. "Mother, we think that Maria is perhaps seven years old, but her aunt, who brought her to Tenza Infant Grange, forgot to provide that information."

"Seven years old seems about right to me," Mother Rosario agreed.

I was then sent to eat lunch, and the food—rice with beans—was delicious. After lunch, the girls went out to a huge yard with basketball courts, where they played many different games. I followed along but was too shy to join in their games. Soon, it was time to go to class. The classrooms were huge—I had never seen anything like them. Most of the teachers were nuns: only three of them were not.

After class, the girls were sent to the bathroom to wash their hands and to take a break. I carefully observed them and did everything they were doing. When it was time for dinner, I was assigned to the seat I would keep for the entirety of my stay. The food for dinner was the same as lunch—rice and beans—and again, it was delicious. Directly after dinner, we were sent to the school's chapel to pray the rosary. After that, we were allowed to go outside to play or do whatever we wanted to do. At about seven o'clock, we washed up and were sent to bed.

There were two large bedrooms at the grange, each with about twenty-five beds. These were placed in a line against the wall and were covered with pink comforters. Mother Rosario led me by the hand to my new bed. "From this moment on, Maria," she said kindly, "you need to remember that this is your bed."

Everything here was so different, and so pretty. I lay down on my bed, feeling tired and happy, and soon fell asleep. Mother Maria Luisa woke me up to change me into a nightgown, but I was so tired that I barely noticed her.

Early the next morning, Mother Rosario came in the room, ringing a bell. All the girls got up and started singing "God Save You, Maria" as they were getting dressed. I put on my uniform, thinking about how happy I was to be in a safe place. I was thankful to Tia Trinita for putting me in the girls' grange.

I quickly learned the morning routine. After we dressed, we waited in line to brush our teeth and wash up. Then, still in a line, we walked back to our room to make our beds. I had never made a bed, but Mother Rosario asked one of the older girls to "keep an eye" on me and to help me until I was comfortable with everything. After our beds were made, we went to the chapel and prayed; after that, we had chores—we swept the halls, cleaned the dining room, washed the bathrooms, and watered the flowers. Then it was time for breakfast. Before eating we thanked God for the food we were about to have, and afterward we prayed again to thank God for the food we had eaten. When breakfast was over, we each washed our dishes and placed them back on the table. From there, we went to our classrooms.

This routine was the same each day, except that on Saturdays we changed our sheets and washed our blankets. There was a small concrete pool outside the building with four washing spots at the corners—that was where we washed our clothes and blankets. In the mornings, we also used the pool for our baths—sometimes that water was very cold. On Saturdays, the Mothers taught us to embroider and to iron our uniforms.

On Sundays, a priest would come to celebrate mass in the grange's chapel, and the boys from another grange would join us. The boys' grange was named Granja del Gran Ciudadano (Grange of the Grand Citizen), it was about a fifteen-minute walk from our grange. About sixty boys came with their teachers, and they always looked good in their uniforms. During each mass, they would sing one song and we girls would sing another. After mass, the teachers would greet each other and spend some time talking together before the boys returned to their grange. We girls had special uniforms for Sundays that were very pretty and looked almost brand-new. Right after mass we had to change out of those uniforms, fold them nicely, and put them in our boxes. Sometimes the older girls helped us to put them away.

After breakfast on Sundays, which was after mass, we went out to play in the patio. The priest would come along and talk to all of us. He was very kind, and he often spent time with the new children, asking their names and where they had come from. Sometimes, he taught us songs.

I was very happy at the Infant Grange. I no longer had to look for sweet potatoes to eat, and all the girls and the nuns were very nice. And I was learning about so many things—some things that I hadn't even known existed.

On visiting day, once a month, relatives would come to see their girls. They often brought sweets, fruit, candy, and clothes to their girls, and some of the girls would share with those who did not have anything.

Mother Maria Luisa called me aside once to ask me about my personal information. She knew my name, of course, and that I had an aunt and was about seven years old. But she wanted to know about the rest of my life. "Do you know where you were born?" she asked.

"Yes, Mother," I answered politely. "I was born in Santa Teresa, Boyacá." Then I told her my parents' names, my aunts' names, and my siblings' names.

"And do you know when you were born?" she asked.

I shook my head. "No, Mother."

She patted my head. "That's all right, Maria," she said. "We know that you arrived here in August 1952. We'll just say you were seven years old on the day that you arrived."

6

By the time I had been living at the grange for a couple of months, everything in my life seemed marvelous, except that I continued to miss Aunt Trinita, my brothers, and baby José. I wanted badly to hear from them and to tell them that I was doing well, even though I missed them a lot.

Each time Señorita Anita came to visit, we girls immediately ran to make a line and greet her. We began to sing her favorite songs: "As of Colors," "Little White Cloth," "Knowing That You Would Return Very Soon," and other beautiful songs. By this time I knew the words to almost all of them. After we sang to her, she thanked us and then sent us to continue our work. Mother Maria Luisa then discussed us with Señorita Anita, telling her whether we were well behaved, if we had been sick, and any other information she could offer, especially about the new girls.

Señorita Anita sent for me during one such visit and examined my whole body. "You look fine, Maria," she pronounced, "but I think I will bring you some vitamins the next time I visit. You look very pale. I don't want you to become anemic."

I was quickly learning the skills that the nuns and other teachers taught us each day. I had been placed in first grade, and I loved my classes. My favorites were grammar and language, and I always got good grades in them; arithmetic, though, was difficult for me. The teachers were really good but very strict;

they sometimes hit the girls' hands with a ruler if they did not do their work.

By the time I'd been in school for about three months, I had learned to write my name—and the other girls' names, too. I could recite the alphabet; I had learned a lot of songs; and I had discovered that I loved to draw. I was quickly becoming accustomed to the school rules and schedule. Mother Maria Luisa sometimes patted my head and told me how beautiful and intelligent I was. Then she'd wink at me and say, "What a pretty name you have, Maria Luisa!" That always made me really happy; something about Mother Maria Luisa—it might have been her smile—reminded me of Tia Trinita.

I was becoming more familiar with the layout of the school, too. In addition to the girls' bedrooms, each teacher had her own room. Señorita Anita's room was very big and nice, although she wasn't there all the time. There was also one for Father Luna, which he used when he visited. And there were rooms set aside for visitors. The kitchen was very large with a lot of windows. The woman who cooked for us was named Julia, and she had a little girl who was about two years old. She was very friendly with everyone.

There were some apple trees on the grounds and lots of pine trees. There was also a large vegetable garden. Farther away from the main building was a large pen with about twenty pigs; the biggest girls helped to feed them. These pigs made a lot of noise. Even I, someone who was used to hearing animal noises, was afraid when they all started squealing—there were so many of them. There also were a lot of cattle on the grange; men from the boys' grange came each day to tend them and bring milk for our breakfast.

When there were no classes, we girls planted seeds and weeded; the biggest girls working with hoes and pickaxes, and the little girls collecting the weeds and throwing them away. All types of plants and flowers grew on the grange, because the climate was very agreeable. The temperature was usually in the sixties, which made the days very pleasant. Sometimes we needed to wear sweaters, but nothing more than that.

It was a mild day in December when Mother Maria Luisa gathered us together and said, "Christmas is coming very soon, so we need to start practicing our Christmas songs and choruses."

The other girls seemed very excited, but I didn't understand. "Mother," I said, "what's Christmas?"

The girls all laughed. Mother laughed gently as well, then quieted them and said, "Christmas is very special, Maria. It's when God's child was born, many years ago. Now, the whole world celebrates his birth, and there are lots of presents, sweets, and candy—but only for good girls who obey and don't fight."

I quickly sat up very straight. "I won't cause any problems, Mother. I'll behave!"

Then we started to practice the songs, accompanying our voices with tambourines, drums, and maracas. We practiced every day so that we could perform perfectly at the Christmas mass.

Another of our projects was to put together a Nativity scene. The biggest girls went to a little mountain near the river to look for moss, sticks, and rocks, which we used as a background. The nuns then brought out the nativity figures, miniature houses, people, and lots of little animals. I was amazed; I had never seen so many pretty little things. The nuns and the big girls spread out the moss and set out the stables and animals. They placed the Virgin Mary and Joseph in a small house toward the back, with a mule and an ox and a crib for baby. They set several angels close by. In another section, the girls made modern towns with the little houses and tracks for the tiny trains. I thought about my brothers and how happy they would have been to see all of these beautiful things. It looked so beautiful, in fact, that I wanted to touch everything, but the big girls wouldn't allow it. "You'll just break it," they said. "But you can stand there and watch us as we add more things." The entire scene was so big that it took them almost a week to finish it. Then, six days before Christmas, they added the Wise Men: Melchior, Gaspar, and Balthazar, who came to bring incense, gold, and myrrh for the baby Jesus.

Señorita Anita came to join us two days before Christmas. As usual, we all ran to greet her with songs. When we finished, she smiled and thanked us. Then she asked, "Are you happy and well behaved, girls?"

"Yes, Señorita Anita," we answered in unison.

Señorita Anita signaled to her driver and assistants, who brought several boxes from the truck, took them inside, and locked them in a storage room. Señorita Anita stayed at the grange that night. We were all very happy, but I think I was especially excited because it was to be my first Christmas; I was filled with joy.

The next day was Christmas Eve. After breakfast, Señorita Anita gathered us around her and said, "It is time to make the tamales. Who would like to help?"

I was the first one to answer, because I wanted to be involved in everything. Señorita Anita taught me to how to wrap each tamale and put it together. I was amazed by the process, because I had never done anything like this in my life. The other girls joined in, and we worked on the tamales until it was time to stop for lunch.

Then we went out to the recess yard to play. Señorita Anita, the nuns, and the big girls went up to the bedrooms after a while, telling us that no one else could come up. We younger children played outside for almost the whole afternoon, until Señorita Anita returned. "We will have a light dinner now," she told us, "because we are going to have another dinner after midnight mass."

At dusk, the nuns gave us sparklers to twirl in our hands while they set off their pretty sparks. I was afraid of them at first, but I gradually got to like them. After a few hours of play, the nuns sent us to bathe ourselves and put on our good uniforms. A priest arrived shortly after that, and he asked us to sing our Christmas songs in front of the Nativity scene; he also told us which songs to sing for the mass. By about 11:30, we were ready and waiting. Señorita Anita, who had put on a pretty red dress, led us all to the chapel to attend the Christmas mass. We sang our songs, and everything was very beautiful. At midnight, one of the girls placed Jesus in the manger while we sang.

When the mass ended, Señorita Anita hugged us one by one and told us "Merry Christmas." The nuns and the priest did the same, and then it was time for our special dinner—tamales, chicken soup, bread, and a caramel dessert with some chocolates.

When we'd finished eating, Señorita Anita stood to address us. "You all have been very well behaved," she said. "And your Christmas carols were a hit. Now, you deserve to go to sleep, but before you do, be sure to check under your beds—because baby Jesus has left you some little presents."

Although we were very excited, we went up to our rooms in an orderly fashion: the older girls went first, the ones in the middle followed, and the little ones came last. Upstairs, I bent down to look under my bed—and there was a package! Inside, I found a toothbrush, toothpaste, a nightgown, a hairbrush, a toy bird that sang when I put water in its base, and some candy. I was thrilled by my first Christmas presents; they all seemed wonderful. I was so happy that I couldn't sleep. I liked the hairbrush most of all, because I'd had to borrow one every time I wanted to brush my hair. All of us were very happy with our different presents.

We all slept until noon the next day, Christmas Day. When we got up, we were allowed to do anything we wanted. Later that afternoon, Señorita Anita had to leave, and we all put our presents away in our boxes. But it had been a wonderful Christmas and a great new experience for me.

Sometimes, on Saturdays, the nuns would take us to a deep river. We got into our bathing suits before leaving the grange, then made the ten-minute walk to the river. The teachers and nuns would watch us while we swam; the older girls also helped them. At first, I was afraid of the river because it was much bigger than the brooks where I used to play with my brothers. I can still remember the loud noise the river made every time its waters splashed against the rocks. Little by little, though, I walked closer to the water. The older girls went fearlessly into the deep water; they liked playing and swimming there. After a day of playing in the river, we would be very tired. When we returned to the grange, I would just say my prayers and go right to sleep.

Every once in a while, relatives would come to visit girls or take them out for a couple of days. New girls arrived sometimes, too. Of course, all visits and new arrivals had to be approved by Señorita Anita. Almost all of the girls got to see their relatives at least occasionally. On Sunday afternoons, when visitors usually arrived, I would wait at the window to see if any of my relatives were among them. They never were.

During the Easter season, the grange was a very quiet place, full of prayers. In May, however, we celebrated the Virgin Maria. We sang beautiful songs like "Ave Maria" and made a wooden altar decked with flowers, which we carried around the grange as we prayed to the Virgin. Some of the girls would have their first communion during this time.

It was Father Luna who administered these first communions. He was very short and skinny, and he always wore a hat. He came to the grange only to do mass and then left the following morning. The nuns, and the other children, treated him like a holy man. I thought that might be because he was the owner of all the granges for children: each was called "The Infant Grange of Father Luna." He did a great deal of good for a great many people.

When my first year of classes at the grange was over, I learned that I had passed to the second grade. It was time for a short break, so we went to visit the boys' grange about fifteen minutes from our school. It was a very big grange, with lots of trees and a lot of classrooms in the school. The river passed close by, and there was a waterfall very high up on the mountain. I remember thinking that the water that fell from it looked extremely white. This grange communicated with the outside world by using an old-fashioned telephone. It hung on the wall, and it had to be cranked to make a connection. The person calling had to hold an earpiece that was attached by a long cord, and it was necessary to speak very loudly.

The Christmas season came again, and this time I knew the songs. We practiced our old favorites, but we learned some new ones, as well. There were other changes at the grange this Christmas, too: we had started hearing rumors that some of the nuns were going to leave and that young women were going to replace them. I was afraid and hoped that didn't mean that Mother Maria Luisa was leaving; I loved her as if she were my aunt Trinita. If she were to leave, it would be like losing my aunt again. Immediately, I went to ask Mother Maria Luisa if the rumors were true.

"Why, yes," she said, looking very surprised that I already knew. "I was about to call all you girls to tell you about it."

When Mother Maria Luisa shared the news that she and Mother Rosario were going to be leaving, all the girls began to sob uncontrollably and begged them not to go. I felt such a great sadness—it occurred to me that everyone I loved disappeared, and I never saw them again. I could not stop crying.

"We're sorry, girls," Mother Maria Luisa said, "but we have no choice. Mother Rosario and I must obey the orders of our superiors. We're leaving a few weeks after Christmas." At that, all the girls began wailing even louder. "Girls, please," Mother Maria Luisa implored us. "Don't worry. Some very good young women are coming to take our places, and I promise that they will take very good care of you."

On Christmas Eve, almost everything was the same as the previous year, except that Señorita Anita wasn't there; she spent each year at a different grange. But we had the same priest who had performed midnight mass the year before, and we sang the same choruses. It all went very well, but I was still sad that Mother Maria Luisa was leaving. After mass, we went to eat dinner, and then the nuns sent us to bed. This year, it was

Mother Maria Luisa who reminded us to look under our beds for presents from the baby Jesus. When I opened mine, I could scarcely believe my eyes. I had received a beautiful doll. It had blue eyes, and—to me—it looked just like a real baby. I hugged it tightly: I couldn't believe I had my very own doll in my arms. How I wished I could share this happiness with Tia Trinita. I missed her, and I missed my brothers and baby José del Carmen, too. We were all very happy with our gifts, but I felt especially happy about getting my beautiful doll.

A few weeks later, Señorita Anita came, this time with two young women. They were the replacements for the nuns. The new señoritas were very young. One was named Maruja, from Venezuela. She was tall, with short black hair and white skin. She seemed very quiet. The other one, who had dark skin, was named Graciela; she would be the new director. She seemed very happy and was almost always laughing. Her hair was long and curly—it looked a lot like mine had before Señorita Anita cut it. Graciela came from Bogotá, the capital.

Señorita Anita introduced us to the women and told us that they would take very good care of us. The next day, a truck came for Mother Maria Luisa and Mother Rosario. It was a very sad good-bye, and we girls cried a lot.

Although we missed the nuns, it seemed at first that the señoritas would be fine replacements. Señorita Graciela asked Señorita Anita for a phonograph, saying that we needed to hear music once in a while. Meanwhile, Señorita Maruja taught us to sew clothing for our dolls. I remember that I made pajamas for my doll, and I showed absolutely everyone that I had learned to sew. I even brought the doll to my classes so that my teachers would see, and it made me very happy. Señorita Maruja also taught us proper manners—how to sit, how to eat, not to put our elbows on the table, and even how to laugh; she was always teaching us something new. We continued with our daily work, but all the girls missed Mother Maria Luisa and Mother Rosario. We wondered how they were doing.

One day, rather unexpectedly, Señorita Anita arrived in her truck. When we hurried out to greet her with a song, we saw her driver lift a box off the truck, and we knew that it was what we had all been waiting for—the phonograph. Señorita Anita had also brought boxes full of clothes and shoes. As soon as we finished singing, Señorita Anita started distributing the shoes. I was very happy with mine—they fit well and were very pretty. Every time that Señorita Anita came to our grange, she brought surprises.

After Señorita Anita left that night, we put on the music and Señorita Graciela started to dance. Soon, she was teaching the older girls. I loved watching them. Hours passed without my realizing it because I was fascinated by the music. We listened to music every night and didn't go to recess or to play with balls anymore; instead, we listened to music and learned to dance.

Señorita Graciela became a great friend to the older girls; sometimes it seemed like she was one of them, and the teachers laughed about that. Señorita Graciela's many sisters and other relatives came to visit her almost every weekend. She also became a great friend of the teachers from the boys' grange, and they began to visit her, too.

Life at the grange seemed to be going very well. I loved my teachers. Then, suddenly, Señorita Graciela began to punish the youngest girls—and that included me—for almost no reason. She would come up to us as we stood in line and pinch us so hard we cried. Then she would ask why we weren't standing up straight or tell us she'd heard us talking in line. The big girls laughed at us when this happened, but we younger girls were becoming very afraid. Señorita Graciela also prohibited us from playing with our dolls.

I continued doing very well in my classes; I liked being in school, and I learned more every day. I also enjoyed drawing—art helped me process my memories and experiences. I drew a picture of three children in a little house and a woman leaving on horseback, which I labeled "My Little House." Then I drew a much larger house with a lot of girls playing in front: across the top of that page, I wrote "My Little Grange." When Señorita Maruja asked us if we wanted to learn to embroider and cross-stitch, I was the first to raise my hand. I loved arts and crafts and liked looking at pictures of cross-stitch embroidery in magazines. Señorita Maruja taught us embroidery almost every Saturday, and it quickly became my favorite class.

One Sunday, Señorita Graciela told us to get our bathing suits because we were going to the river to swim. We all ran very happily to the river. At first, I was a little afraid because the sound of the water was so strong, but I gradually lost my fear and played with the other girls on the shore. The older girls were swimming in the deep parts of the river and playing in the water with Señorita Graciela. We could tell that Señorita Graciela was telling secrets to the big girls—she was whispering to them and they were laughing. Suddenly, they came toward us and grabbed a little girl who was playing with me. They brought her out to the deepest part of the river and started to submerge her in the water. The girl begged them to stop and tried to hit them with her hands, but they kept dunking her under the water. Each time they did, they'd laugh, They kept on dunking her until she seemed to lose consciousness. Then they finally took her to the shore, where she vomited up river water. Then they grabbed me and forced me to the same part of the river. I screamed, knowing what they were going to do. They dunked me over and over again. I kept yelling at them to stop, and I swallowed a lot of water. More water went up my nose each time they dunked me under. I fought with my hands, but it was impossible to get away from them—they were too strong, and there were too many of them. It was the most horrible moment of my life: I thought I was going to die.

I don't know when they took me out of the water; the next thing I remember is waking up on the shore with an aching head and vomit on my face. I heard some girls crying, but others were cracking up, laughing. Looking around me, I saw other little girls lying on the ground, half-conscious. A few big girls who had not taken part in the "game" came to comfort me.

"Those girls and Señorita Graciela are very bad," one whispered to me. But I knew they wouldn't tell anyone. They were afraid, too.

Finally, Señorita Graciela said it was time to go back to the grange. As we walked, she warned us not to talk about what had happened. "I just hate gossiping girls," she said. "If any of you say anything about the games in the water, you'll get a *huge* punishment."

It wasn't long after that day that the older girls started to fight among themselves. They were divided into two groups—one group was made up of Señorita Graciela's friends, and the other of those who feared and disliked her. They fought all the time, even when they were standing in line. Señorita Graciela usually ignored their fighting, but one day she told them to stop. "This is exactly what I expected from a bunch of street girls from Bogotá."

A couple of the older girls angrily told Señorita that they hadn't come from the street. "I don't come from the street, either," I piped up. I knew immediately that I shouldn't have said anything. "Go out into the yard, Maria," she ordered, pinching me as hard as she could, "and kneel there while holding a brick in each hand."

She pointed at the other girls who were there, too, but only those who were not in her group. "You others can do the same."

I wished that Señorita Maruja could help us, but she didn't seem to realize what was going on. The next Sunday, when some relatives arrived with little gifts for their girls, Señorita Graciela told them they had to leave without seeing their girls. The relatives complained, but they couldn't do anything about it—Señorita Graciela was the director, after all.

At night, Señorita Graciela continued teaching us to dance—she had bought a lot of records that looked like thick plates. We all danced every night—even the cook joined us. I loved dance. She also taught us more songs to sing to Señorita Anita. On her next visit, Señorita Anita noticed our new songs right away and told us that the songs were very beautiful. Then she asked Señorita Graciela how we were behaving. We were surprised when she replied "very well"—we thought we must have deserved all the punishment she meted out.

We youngest girls asked Señorita Maruja if we could play with our dolls during recess time.

"Of course you can," she answered.

But Señorita Graciela heard her response and said, "No, they can't. I told them they couldn't play with their dolls."

They started fighting about it, and the little girls were crying because it had been months since we had played with our dolls. In the end, Señorita Maruja won the argument—we could play with our dolls. At recess time, we ran to the boxes where our dolls and toys were kept. We opened them eagerly and found—nothing. We were frightened and went to ask the señoritas.

"I don't know where your dolls are," Señorita Graciela insisted.

"I'm sorry, girls," Señorita Maruja said more kindly, "but I don't know anything."

We began to cry about the loss of our dolls. I sobbed and sobbed, because I had lost the most beautiful thing I had ever owned. I had only had it for about eight months, and now it was gone. I was very sad about everything that had happened to us since the Mothers had left.

When Señorita Anita returned, one of the girls told her that we had lost our dolls. "What does she mean, they lost their dolls?" Señorita Anita asked the señoritas.

Señorita Graciela shook her head disgustedly. "They are very disorganized girls. They don't know where to find their dolls."

Señorita Anita pursed her lips and looked at us sternly. "I'm very disappointed in you girls," she said. "You will have no recess for one week. Instead, you will pray the rosary during that time."

7

Despite Señorita Graciela's unkindness, I still enjoyed life at the grange. I continued to do well in my studies. My teachers said that I was very smart and learned quickly. I could also do embroideries of things like little animals and flowers. Instead of going out to play at recess, I stayed inside and embroidered. Señorita Maruja gave me a piece of white linen I could make into an embroidery sampler with my name on it. I happily started embroidering it with a lot of trim and examples of every stitch I had learned. When I'd finished, Señorita Maruja did the hem with crochet and promised to teach me how to do that, too.

I had friends at the grange now. My best friends were Tina and Gloria; we were almost always together. When their families came to visit them, they invited me to join in, and their families shared with me the things that they had brought for their girls.

One day, much to my dismay, it was decided that we would go to the river again. When I heard this, I got so afraid that I got a stomachache. We little girls all started to cry and said that we didn't want to go. But it was useless to protest. Señorita Graciela made us go. I wished that Aunt Trinita would come and take me away, but I knew that was impossible. I hadn't heard from my family for three years.

As we climbed down to the river, I was crying and shaking in fear. As always, the big girls threw themselves into the deepest part of the river to swim, but we little ones didn't even want to play with the shells or little fish. Then one of the biggest ones started throwing water at us. Her friends grabbed us and dragged us to the deep part to dunk us like they had the last time. But this time, another group of big girls swam out to stop them. These other girls took us back to the shore, where they started fighting with the girls who wanted to dunk us. The fight was so intense that even Señorita Graciela was unnerved. She blew her whistle and ordered everyone out of the water. "Everyone! Back to the grange! Now!" she said shakily.

On the way back, the girls who had saved us said that they would always be our defenders, and I was very happy about their bravery. But we still wondered what Señorita Graciela was going to do. We found out soon enough.

That night, about midnight, Señorita Graciela woke up several girls, including me. "Go down to the yard behind the bathrooms," she ordered us, "and kneel there. This is your punishment for behaving badly at the river."

We made our way as best as we could in the dark. I was shaking because I was scared and half-asleep, but I knelt with the others in the yard. The older girls who were kneeling there said that no one from Señorita Graciela's group was being punished, even though they were the ones who had started the problem. Still, we stayed on our knees.

After about ten minutes, we saw white shadows and something that looked like horns; the shapes were making horrible noises as they approached us. Terrified, we screamed like savages. Then the biggest girl confronted one of these white shadows, pulling off what turned out to be a sheet to reveal the person underneath. With that, all the shadows ran away and disappeared.

"Don't be afraid," the big girl said. "I saw who was under that sheet—it was Blanca." Blanca was a girl from Señorita Graciela's group. There were no monsters, just bullies. "Just calm down," she said. "We're okay."

Soon Señorita Graciela came to tell us that we could go to sleep. "Next time we go to the river," she warned, "I expect you to behave yourselves."

"But Señorita," I said bravely, "I didn't do anything."

She scowled at me, an expression I could see even in the darkness. "You and the other little girls were the cause of the fight, so you're just as guilty as the others."

Soon it was time for Christmas again, my third Christmas at the grange.

"Who do you think brings the Christmas gifts?" one of the little girls asked me.

"Jesus does," I answered.

She laughed. "Don't believe that! Señorita Anita and the director bring them, and the big girls put them under the beds."

"That's a lie!" I said, "Mother Maria Luisa doesn't tell lies, and she said it was Jesus."

The girl shrugged. "If you don't believe me, just pay attention to what the director and the big girls are doing on Christmas Eve."

"No!" I insisted. "You're lying!"

I felt a little older now, and I had learned a lot. I was becoming wary. I didn't let the big girls, who were about sixteen or seventeen, hit me. I thought that when the girls were eighteen, their families brought them back home. Then I realized that if

Aunt Trinita wouldn't come for me until I turned eighteen, I still had eight years left.

One Saturday, Father Luna came to speak with the teachers and with Señoritas Graciela and Maruja. He also spoke with the big girls in private—I thought he was telling them to be good. He spent the night at the grange, and we had to maintain absolute silence—especially in the morning—so we wouldn't wake him up too early. Children from other granges and people from the village came to see him hold mass in the cafeteria, a big room full of plants and flowers: it was the only room large enough to hold everyone. As at every mass, the boys sang a song and then the girls. Father Luna congratulated us for singing so beautifully and gave us his blessing. After mass and breakfast, Father Luna left. We scattered to put our uniforms away and make our beds.

After that, Señorita Graciela told us that we were to have lunch on top of a hill. She said we were going to enjoy it because we could slide down the hill after we ate. We all got very excited. Lunch included lots of pasta, as well as brown sugar to make a caramel dessert. When we got to the top of the hill, we started a campfire and placed the brown sugar near it so it would start melting. We ate lunch while the dessert was being prepared. It took almost two hours before it was ready, and it had to be stirred constantly so it did not stick to the pan. After lunch, we slid down the hill, as Señorita Graciela said we could. It was fun for a while, but after a couple of times some girls got dizzy and started vomiting. After a while, Señorita Graciela asked us to get in line because the dessert was almost ready. We all received a little bit of it in our hands, and then we had to pat for a couple of minutes until the color changed from brown to white—that meant that it was ready to be eaten. It was delicious.

We still wanted to play on the hill, so Señorita Graciela suggested that we younger girls sit on denim blankets and let the older girls push us down the hill. I did not want to do that; those games always scared me because the older girls could get too rough. Some of the little girls agreed to the idea, but after a few minutes they were crying because they'd gotten hurt or were feeling nauseated. Fortunately, none of the older girls got into fights that day. Everyone played happily.

Some of our teachers were getting ready for their vacations, so Señorita Graciela called the teachers from another grange to help us put up some swings in our yard. The trees she chose for the swings were the biggest and the tallest on the hill. We all were eager to see those swings, but I was sure that I was the most excited of all. I had always loved the idea of having them. Once the swings were ready, the teachers and Señorita Graciela tried them out first. They laughed and seemed to enjoy themselves. Once they had tested the swings, they left us alone in the yard. The older girls grabbed the swings first, but I finally got a turn. One of the older girls started pushing me really hard, but I didn't like swinging so high. I yelled at her to stop, but she did not listen to me. She kept on pushing me higher and higher, and because I was scared, I just let go of the rope. I landed hard on my back and went tumbling down the hill. It felt like my back was on fire, and it was hard to breathe. When I'd tumbled to the bottom of the hill, one of the big girls ran to help me. When she saw my back, she got really scared. A large patch of skin had been scraped off, and it was bleeding heavily. Back at the grange, a teacher cleaned my back and put medicine and bandages on it, but that did not stop the pain. To make matters worse, Señorita Graciela was nowhere to be found. I was given a pill for the pain, and soon Señorita Graciela returned, carrying my dinner. "Don't worry, Maria," she said. "You'll get better soon. But don't use the swings anymore." I finally fell asleep, but kept waking up throughout the night. The pain in my back was so strong that I felt it all over my body.

The next day I couldn't get up because my whole body hurt. I thought a lot about my family, how much I missed them, and how lonely I was feeling. Señorita Maruja changed my bandages and gave me another pain pill. She patted my head and played with my hair.

Another teacher came and asked Señorita Maruja about my family. "Do they know what happened?"

Señorita Maruja shook her head. "I don't know where Maria's family is."

I felt sad when I heard that, more than ever before. But the days passed, and my back got better, little by little, until finally it did not hurt me anymore.

The teachers left for vacation, and only Señorita Graciela, Señorita Maruja, and the cook, Señora Julia—a lovely lady who was like a mother to many of us—stayed behind.

Christmas Eve arrived. That morning was just like any other, except that a truck full of boxes arrived. Señora Julia gave us lots of bags and candy to put in them; this was for us. That night, as usual, the older girls and the teachers disappeared for a long time, reappearing for mass. Señorita Anita could not come that year, but we had our traditional firecrackers and supper of tamales—we had fun that night! The songs during mass sounded beautiful, and when one of the girls placed baby Jesus in his crib, we all looked at the figure with tenderness. At the end of mass, we hugged each other and wished each other a merry

Christmas. I was very eager to open my present that year. I received a green plastic watch, which I thought was beautiful. I also got a small purse and lots of clothes. It was my third Christmas at the grange, and I enjoyed it a little bit more each year.

After the holiday season had ended, and we were back to our regular routine, Señorita Graciela announced that we were going on a field trip. "We're going to walk to the other side of the river," she told us, "where we'll pick lots of fruit. And on our way back here, we'll go past a very tall train bridge—that should be exciting for all of us."

I was not excited; anything that had to do with the river scared me. I wanted to stay behind, but Señorita Graciela would not allow it. "Only those who have been sick with the flu may stay behind," she said, and I knew I couldn't argue with her. And so we left for the other side of the river, approximately fifty girls in all. We looked for an area of the river with big rocks to walk across, but we got wet anyway. Once on the other side of the river, we found a path to a grange with many apple and pear trees. We picked fruit and then sat down to eat it. As we sat, we watched the butterflies and birds. Many of the girls were surprised to see all these creatures, but not me—I had often seen such things when I lived with my family. When it was time to return to our grange, we followed the train tracks to the bridge. I was really scared to cross it, but I tried to hide my fear. The bridge was very tall and narrow—about sixty feet off the ground and one hundred feet long. Although I had been impressed by its height from far away, I had never imagined crossing it: I was afraid of heights. Señorita Graciela and some of the older girls got on their knees and placed their ears to the ground to check if the train was near. There were many trees and curves on the mountain, so we could not see if the train was coming or not. "I don't hear anything," Señorita Graciela announced. "It's safe for us to cross the bridge." Señorita Graciela and the older girls led the way, and we younger ones followed. We crossed the bridge on our hands and knees because the space between the tracks was so wide that we were afraid of falling off the high bridge and into the river.

The older girls were almost halfway to the other side, and the younger girls had just started to crawl onto the tracks, when suddenly we heard a loud noise that sounded like a train. We looked behind us; it wasn't a train, fortunately, but it was a car that a train conductor had sent out ahead to check for branches on the tracks. When the men in the car saw us, they yelled and whistled loudly to get our attention.

"Come back this way!" one yelled at us. "The train is coming very soon!" All the girls were so scared that they started to crawl back as fast as they could. The men continued to yell to us, telling us that we should go back to the beginning of the tracks and quickly throw ourselves off the sides. One of the men called out to us, as we hastily crawled backward, asking us what school we attended. Although it seemed an odd question at the time, one of the big girls answered that we belonged to the Infant Grange of Father Luna. Thankfully, we all managed to safely reach the beginning of the tracks and jump off. Only a few minutes later, the train passed us.

Señorita Graciela realized that if it hadn't been for those men, we would have been killed. She suggested that we go back by the same route that we took to get there. We all breathed a sigh of relief that we wouldn't be crossing the train bridge again, and we walked very cautiously on our way back. We had been saved by the grace of God.

That night we all went to bed very quiet and full of thoughts. I was thankful to God for saving my life. I was also thinking about my aunt Trinita and my brother Avelino, and what their reactions might be if they knew all the things that I was experiencing.

Señorita Anita came to visit us the next day. This time, she didn't praise our singing; she seemed to be very upset. She pushed past us and went into the school.

After a while, Señorita Maruja came out and spoke to us. "Señorita Anita has left, and she has taken Señorita Graciela with her." Señorita Maruja quickly scanned our faces, and she seemed very concerned. "Girls, why didn't one of you tell me about what happened on the train bridge?" We all were very quiet, and Señorita Maruja seemed to understand. "You don't have to be afraid of Señorita Graciela anymore," she assured us. "She will never return to the grange."

That news made me so happy that I thought that my heart was going to jump out of my body! I was so glad to hear this because Graciela was a bully. I remembered the men asking us where we were from and knew who had alerted Señorita Anita.

"Just imagine what could have happened!" Señorita Maruja kept saying. She told us things would be different now. We were once again allowed to play with our toys. I wished I still had my doll, but it had never been returned. I chose to get busy with my embroidery instead.

A couple of days later, Señorita Anita and Father Luna came to visit us, along with a woman we didn't recognize. We all got on our knees to receive Father Luna's blessing, and we sang Señorita Anita's favorite songs. This time she told us that she was pleased to hear us sing, and then she introduced our new director, Señorita Mariela. She was tall and very pretty, with short hair. Señorita Anita and Señorita Maruja took our new director on a tour of the grange. Meanwhile, Father Luna asked the older girls why we had been crossing such a dangerous bridge that day.

"Señorita Graciela ordered us to cross it, Father," one girl offered. "She thought that it was the best way to go back to the grange."

Father Luna put his hands to his head in a gesture of despair. "You girls are lucky to be alive," he said, his voice quavering. Then he gave us a stern look. "You are never to go to the river again."

Father Luna and Señorita Anita left the next day, warning us to behave well for the new director. They promised to visit us more often.

Señorita Mariela was a very good director, but she also was very strict. She made strong demands of us, but she was not crazy, like Señorita Graciela had sometimes seemed. Little by little, I grew to like her.

Soon it was the month of May—the month of the Virgin Mary—and Señorita Mariela asked if there were any girls who had not made their first communion. I was the first one to raise my hand, and several other little girls followed my lead.

"You must start by learning about catechism," Señorita Mariela said.

"But we already know all the prayers for the catechism," I told her.

Señorita Mariela's eyebrows shot up in surprise. "Then why haven't you made your first communions?"

No one spoke. We didn't want to say anything against Señorita Graciela, who had never mentioned it during the year she had been with us.

Señorita Mariela nodded her head. "Ah, I see," she said knowingly. "Well, you still will need to study a little bit more so you can really be ready for your first communion."

Later, when the relatives came to visit, she asked them to bring appropriate clothing for first communion—a white dress and shoes. The relatives were very happy for their girls, so they promised to help in any way possible. I stayed quiet: I did not have any relatives to ask for a dress and shoes.

When the other girls' dresses started to arrive, I decided to tell Señorita Mariela that I had been at the grange for many years but no one had ever come to visit me.

"I do have relatives," I said, "but I don't know where they are."

She patted my head. "Oh, poor Maria Luisa. Don't worry; someday they'll come to see you."

Her words made me cry—no one had ever told me that.

Señorita Mariela hugged me to her. "You don't need to cry anymore. A few of the other girls haven't received their dresses either. I'll ask Señorita Anita to buy them." She just hoped that Señorita Anita would come soon, because we only had two weeks before our big day.

But Señorita Anita did not come. When the truck came to bring our monthly groceries, Señorita Anita was not on it. So Señorita Marielita gave the driver a letter, telling him to get it to Señorita Anita as soon as possible.

Two days later, Señorita Anita arrived at the grange with yards of white silk and lots of lace. She had also brought a seamstress with her to make our dresses, and she measured our feet to buy our shoes. Before she left, she said, "I want all of you to behave. As for those who are to do your first communion, get ready to confess your sins."

The part about confessing did not sound good to me, especially if I had to do it with Father Agudelo, one of the priests who performed the mass when Father Luna was not there. I used to make fun of him when he sang during mass, until my friends told me that mocking a priest was a mortal sin. I felt that I really needed to confess that, but was reluctant to do so—especially to Father Agudelo himself.

The seamstress started working on our dresses. I was the first one to be measured. I asked for a very wide skirt with plenty of ruffles. She looked at me, smiling. "I'll make it just the way you want it."

I hoped this was true. I remembered Grandma and how she had taken my first pretty dresses and made them ugly by attaching the red fabric. I desperately wanted a pretty dress. On Saturday morning, the day before our first communion, the seamstress asked us to try on our dresses. Just as she had promised, mine had a wide skirt, with lots of frills and ruffles. I also had a stiff layer of netting that held the shape of the skirt. I had never seen such a beautiful dress.

That afternoon Father Agudelo came to the grange. Señorita Mariela asked us to make a line to confess our sins. I intentionally placed myself last. Señorita took my arm and asked me to be the first one, as I was the oldest of the group. This made me very nervous. Father Agudelo sat in the confession room and called me in. He said, "Ave Maria." And I answered, "She was found without any sins."

Then he asked me to confess all my sins. And that is what I did. I had confessed about my swearing to my classmates and about the times that I stole goodies from them. At the very end, I haltingly told him that I had a mortal sin to confess.

Very calmly, he told me, "Say it, so that you can be forgiven in the name of God."

I took a deep breath, and then I told him that when he sang during mass, I made fun of him, telling the other girls that he sounded like a cow.

He remained quiet for a few seconds. Then it sounded as if he were coughing or trying to blow his nose, but I soon realized that he was trying to hold back his laughter. "Do not worry," he said. "All of your sins are forgiven."

8

Señorita Mariela said that the girls who were going to make first communion the next day must stay isolated from the other girls. "You must stay quiet, too," she cautioned us, "because otherwise you might commit sins and not be able to make your first communion tomorrow." It was understood that if we mingled with the other girls we could commit sins by possibly getting into fights or swearing.

Señorita Anita came in and gently hugged us. She told us that our first communion was very important, because it meant that we were going to receive God in the holy host bread. She also gave us boxes that she had brought for us, in which she'd placed shoes and accessories for us to wear the next day. My shoes were gorgeous, and I couldn't wait for the next day.

After dinner, we were all sent to the chapel to pray the rosary. Then we were to take a bath and go to sleep. The older girls tried to tease us by saying they had extra work because of us: they had to clean the dining room for the celebration. I didn't listen. As excited as I was about my first communion, I soon fell asleep.

The next morning, Señorita Maruja told those of us taking communion not to eat or drink anything. The older girls helped us to get dressed in our new dresses and put veils on our heads. I felt like a mummy—the crinoline was so stiff and the dress was so long that I could barely walk. The girls all told me how pretty I looked, though, and that made me feel very happy.

I could not walk down the stairs, so the older girls carried me down. All eight of us girls who were taking our first communion stood together, and Señorita Anita gave us a white book and a candle.

"You all look very pretty on the outside," she told us, "and your souls should be just as pretty on the inside. Be good girls, especially with your neighbors, and follow the Ten Commandments. You are the mothers of tomorrow, and you will need to learn how to set a good example for your children."

The entire patio beside the dining room was filled with white flowers that we called margaritas, and the altar was filled with white lilies. Everything looked clean and hopeful. Then people started to arrive, including the families of some of the girls. The boys from the other grange came with their directors. Some of them were also taking their first communion, and they were dressed all in white and carrying lilies and a candle. Señorita Anita hugged them and then placed them in a line, and she spoke to them the same words she had spoken to us. Next, Señorita Maruja lit our candles, and Father Agudelo began the ceremony. All the boys and girls sang throughout the service. Everything was going beautifully, until one of the girls leaned her candle too close to the girl in front of her. The girl's dress caught on fire, but Señorita Maruja quickly ran over and put it out; the girl wasn't hurt, thank God.

The boys and girls continued to sing; it was like celestial magic. When it was time for communion, we all stepped up to take the bread. The priest told me to open my mouth and stick out my tongue. I took my first communion and then walked back to my seat and thanked God for everything he had given me. I thanked him for my little grange, and for the fact that I didn't have to be hungry anymore. I thanked him for allowing me to learn how to read and write, and for making me feel well protected. I felt very peaceful and happy inside. Then I asked God to protect my brothers and my family, especially my aunt Trinita. How I wished they could have been there with me.

At breakfast after the mass, all of the girls who had taken communion went to sit at the table with Señorita Anita and the superiors. That was a great honor for us, and Señorita Anita congratulated us for completing such an important event in our lives.

And so the months continued to pass by, and we learned more and more in our classes. I continued to enjoy my embroidery class, and I learned how to combine the colors of the threads to make lifelike pictures. Señorita Anita sometimes brought white blouses so that we could embroider pictures on them. We never went back to the river again, and that made me very happy, too. By the end of that August, I had spent almost four years at my little grange, and I felt much older than when I'd arrived. Then, I could barely see my face in the bathroom mirror; now I was so tall that I could see only my waist.

Later that month Señorita Maruja gathered us all together and told us that she had to leave our grange for good. She told us that she had to go back home to Venezuela. She said she wanted us to behave and not to forget her teachings about humanity and about respecting each other. We felt very sad that she was leaving, because we loved her so much.

"But Señorita," I asked, "who will teach us embroidery if you go?"

She smiled warmly at me. "You don't need to learn more. You know enough already. In fact, you know enough to teach the other girls." Everyone laughed at that, including me, but I was proud that she'd praised me in this way.

No one was sent to replace Señorita Maruja, but Señorita Mariela—or Señorita Marielita, as we affectionately called her—assigned a different older girl each week to help take care of the little ones. There were still three other teachers, but they had many other tasks and went home to their families on the weekends. Other new little girls kept arriving, and it reminded me of when I first arrived. I consoled them when they cried by telling them that their parents would come to visit them or by inviting them to play with me.

Some of the older girls had reached eighteen years of age, and so it was time for them to leave. This made me sad because I knew that once they left I would never see them again. As I grew older, they didn't tease me as they had when I was little, and I loved them like sisters. I remember the day I followed a couple of them when they took a walk on a Sunday afternoon. They had hidden cups under their uniforms, and I was curious about what they planned to do. They walked into the farm where the cows were kept. There, they started to milk the cows in order to sneak a glass for themselves. As I watched them, I remembered my two aunts and my mother milking the cows at Grandma's house. I started giggling, and when the girls turned around and saw me, they laughed, too. Then they offered me a cup of milk—it was delicious straight from the cow. I think they offered it to me because they were afraid that I might tell on them, but I didn't care; it felt good to be included. We drank the milk and kept our secret to ourselves.

On my fourth Christmas at the grange, a group of us were told to go to the river to get moss for the manger scene. It was the first time we'd been back to the river since we were forbidden to play there, and I was a little nervous, but we had a great time. Maybe that was partly because we were gathering moss and not going swimming, but it was a nice adventure this time.

Señorita Anita brought new pieces for us to add to our Nativity scene, as she usually did. We made little towns and added little houses and animals and many beautiful decorations—it looked better every year. Señorita Anita was not able to be with us on Christmas, and this year Father Luna was there for the service, instead of Father Agudelo. We sang and ate our special dinner, and then we went up to our rooms to open our gifts. This year, I didn't get toys; I got something of much more value to me—a collection of embroidery books and painting books, as well as a lot of clothes. I was happy, because this was exactly what I needed. Christmas always was exciting for me at the grange, maybe because I had never celebrated one at home. This year was just as marvelous as the three that preceded it.

Shortly after the beginning of the new year, Señorita Marielita told us that she was going to create a "Wall of Honor," and that the girls who behaved best would have their names put on that wall. My name was among the first ten she placed there. It made me very proud, and I determined to behave even better.

Señorita Anita came to visit, bringing a little white puppy that looked like a big cotton ball—a French poodle. She stayed with us for over a week this time, and she checked our ears, our skin, and our teeth. She noticed that some of us had cavities, so she told her driver to bring a dentist to the grange; he came the very next day. I had never been to see a dentist, and so I had no idea what to expect. When he checked my teeth, he told me that he had to remove one of my molars and one of my other teeth because they were so rotten that he couldn't fix them.

He started to give me a shot of anesthetic, but when I saw the needle I started to scream. Señorita Anita and one of the big girls helped to calm me down. Although the dentist gave me the Novocain, I still felt a lot of pain when he extracted my teeth.

Afterward, I was given some pills and taken upstairs to the bedroom, where I fell asleep. When I woke up the next day, the pain was horrible and my face was swollen—I cried all day long. Señorita Anita gave me saltwater to use as a gargle to calm the swelling, and she told me that I'd be okay in a few days. Thankfully, she was right.

A few months later, Señorita Marielita told us that she was going to be away for a month, visiting her family. She told us to behave and that someone was coming to replace her for the time being. Every time this happened, I would get nervous. I didn't know how the new person was going to treat us.

When Señorita Marielita's replacement arrived, I was relieved. She seemed to be very gentle and good. She was beautiful, with long, thick hair that she wore in braids wrapped around her head. Her name was Señorita Mercedes, and she told us that her brother was a teacher in a boys' grange in another area. She was a wonderful singer and taught us many songs. On Saturdays and Sundays, she liked to take us to eat lunch at a place that was close to the grange's animals. She seemed to be a wonderful replacement.

Then one day, when it was almost lunchtime and we were all in line, Señorita Mercedes walked briskly up to us and said very loudly, "Which of you girls stole twenty pesos from my room?" I could tell she was furious: she stood rigid, tapping her foot and breathing hard. "No one is going to eat," she threatened, "until the money appears." We all stood quietly; no one volunteered information. After a few minutes, Señorita Mercedes whispered something to a couple of the older girls, and they pointed to another girl, whose name was Olivia. Señorita Mercedes checked Olivia's pockets—and there were the twenty pesos. Señorita Mercedes whispered to the older girls again, and they dragged Olivia to the kitchen, where we could hear her screaming as if she were going to die. A few teachers came rushing in, having heard those horrible screams, but they were too late. Señorita Mercedes and the girls had put Olivia's hands on the fire, and she was severely burned. When the other teachers ran into the kitchen, Olivia was screaming and rolling around on the floor. They ran to get butter to put on her hands for the pain, but she wouldn't let them touch her. Everyone was afraid—her hands smelled like burned meat. The teachers were furious with Señorita Mercedes and the girls who had helped her do such a thing. They finally managed to put a cream on Olivia's hands, but she kept screaming until the cook brought a pot of cold water and they put her hands into it. Then they told us to leave, and they carried Olivia to the nearest bedroom. Some girls who saw Olivia said her skin had fallen off, and all that was left was black. We were called back to the lunchroom, but even thinking about Olivia's hands caused us to lose our appetites.

Despite their anger with Señorita Mercedes, the teachers decided not to take Olivia into town to a doctor; instead, they said they would heal her wounds with ointments and bandages. Poor Olivia didn't stop crying until she finally fell asleep. After the third day, we were allowed to visit her. When I saw her with so many bandages, I started crying. I felt especially bad for her because I knew that, like me, that poor girl had no family and nobody to visit her.

Although the teachers continued taking care of Olivia, she was getting worse. There was a rotten smell coming out of her room, and Olivia couldn't eat or talk. They decided to take her to the nearest hospital, which was located in Alban. They placed her in the care of the hospital staff, who called Señorita Anita with the information. First, Señorita Anita went to the hospital to check on Olivia, and then she came straight to the grange to make sure the other girls were all right and to tell Señorita Mercedes that she had to leave immediately. Señorita Anita brought Olivia back to the grange a few days later. I visited Olivia at her bedside, and she was well enough to laugh with me for a while. I hugged her and told her how sorry I was for what had happened to her. She admitted to me that she had taken the money, but she had never expected to receive such a severe punishment. She would never, she said, ever steal again—not even something as small as a needle.

The other girls went to visit her then, and they joked with her to make her feel better. We were all happy that she was recovering, but her hands still looked very sore. The nerves showed through the thin skin, looking like the roots of a plant pulled from the ground. Olivia couldn't move her hands or fingers at this point—and she never fully regained their use. When Señorita Marielita came back, she was very sad to see the burned girl. She started to cry, and the older girls who had helped to burn Olivia looked very regretful. Those who had been on the Wall of Honor were immediately removed.

After a few days, Señorita Anita left and everything seemed to return to normal. One day not long after that, my friends and I decided to explore the drainage system that led from the bathrooms. We followed a big tube that came out of the building and over a hill. We went over the hill and found where the drain eventually emptied. Near there, we saw many beautiful flowers called "flowers of paradise," but even though they were very pretty, the area smelled horrible. We picked some flowers for Señorita Marielita, but one of the girls tripped and fell in the mud. We helped pull her out, but in doing so, we all got very dirty. As we walked into the grange, some of the other girls whispered about how horrible we smelled. When we gave the flowers to Señorita Marielita, she scolded us for having gone to that place without permission and told us to go take a bath. But then she started laughing, and the other girls joined in her laughter, because they all knew that we weren't covered in mud; we were covered in the sewage from our bathroom.

At the beginning of each month, one or two food trucks always came to the grange to supply us with different types of beans and rice. I was waiting in line to get my lunch when the truck showed up one day. I watched the men unloading the truck, but I couldn't see their faces. When they had finished, they came to the cafeteria to get something to eat. As I walked past the men sitting at a table, I realized that one of them was my cousin Desiderio. He was the last person that I wanted to see! Many horrible memories from the past flashed through my head. My hands were trembling, and I wanted to run out of the room. Fortunately, he didn't recognize me. I realized then that I must look very different from the last time he saw me. It made me sad that he wasn't looking for me, though—it meant that Aunt Trinita had not sent a message with him. I thought she must have forgotten me, but then I realized that she probably hadn't told him where I was in order to protect me.

On Señorita Anita's next visit to the grange, she shared some news with us. "I'm going to take Olivia with me today," she explained. "An American family wants to adopt her. They've promised to see to it that she has surgery on her hands." Olivia still had trouble moving her hands and fingers—she couldn't even hold a spoon. We were happy for her, but Olivia was sad; she had been at the grange for over seven years, and she felt that it was her home. It was very hard for us, too, to see Olivia go away, but we knew it was the best for her. Maybe she would have a better future because of it.

Several months later, Father Agudelo invited us to join in the festivities that take place at the seminary, such as fruit picking and kite flying. Everyone was excited about taking a trip. We packed up some things—balls, kites, a radio, and a blanket—and then waited patiently for the truck to come for us. When it arrived, I saw to my horror that the boy opening the doors to let us on the truck was Desiderio. I started to shake and got very nervous.

"Señorita Marielita," I said, my voice quavering, "I feel sick to my stomach. I'd rather not go on the trip."

Señorita Marielita laughed good-naturedly. "Why, Maria Luisa, you've been more excited than anyone, ever since this trip was planned. Just pull yourself together."

I got into the truck with my legs trembling. I walked to the back, past Desiderio, but I didn't look at him. We all sang as we rode along, and I tried to join in and be happy. We arrived at the seminary and entered a huge house. The priests gave us drinks and fruits and guided us to the backyard, where we could eat and play. After we all ate the fruit, we played ball and flew kites. Desiderio and the truck's driver played ball with the older girls. I thought again that it was strange that he didn't recognize me, and I even considered approaching him to ask him about our family. It would be good to know how they were doing, but I was fearful of getting close to him and even more fearful of talking to him. We rode back to the grange later that night. I was so tired that I fell sleep on the way, and when I woke up it was time to get off the truck. I realized that as worried as I had been that Desiderio might recognize me and try to hurt me again, he thought that I was just another girl from the grange. After that trip, I never saw my cousin Desiderio again.

9

Señorita Anita said that someone had given her a house that was located fifteen minutes away from our grange. She was thinking of making another home for little girls there, but there was only a walking path to that land—there were no highways or roads for a car. So Señorita Anita and Señorita Marielita decided that we would have to build a road so we could more easily reach the house. We each were given a tool—there were hoes, picks, rakes, and wheelbarrows—and told we were responsible for it.

I was given a hoe, which I really liked. It was like my toy. We started the road right where our basketball court ended and went in the direction of the house. At first it was easy, because the ground was flat and had only grass and rocks. We were supposed to put the rocks to the side and fill in any holes in the ground.

Over time, our work got harder and harder because there were more rocks, more holes to cover, and even trees to be removed. The trees were small, but it was still a lot of work to cut them out and drag them aside. We often cut ourselves on the tools, and we dropped rocks on our feet and got a lot of bruises. At the end of the day, we were so exhausted that we barely had the strength to pray. When we returned to the grange, we were so soiled that we looked like bears. We would take a bath, have dinner, pray an Ave Maria, and then go straight to sleep. We worked on the road every day after school.

Sometimes, the teachers would come to see us work and give us advice on how to do the job, but they never used the tools themselves. After a couple of months, it was vacation time—but when we had vacations, we worked even harder. We would start very early in the morning, come back for lunch, and then go back to work on the road until very late.

We didn't have time to rehearse any Christmas songs that year, but we sang the Christmas songs that we already knew. We had a great dinner, and then we went up to our rooms and opened our presents. Even though I was getting older, opening presents was my favorite part of Christmas. This was my fifth Christmas at the grange, and I still hadn't heard anything about my family. Even though I hadn't seen them for five years, I missed them just as much as I had on the first day. I never lost hope of seeing them again. I often thought of my little brother, Eliecer, and my older brother, Avelino. And I thought of my aunts, Trinita and Conchita.

Once our Christmas celebration was over, we went back to work on the road. Sometimes there were little hills, and we had to use the hoes and shovels to flatten them. Further on, there was a small river that we crossed by jumping on top of the rocks. We had to put down a lot of rocks until the surface was even—it took us about a month of tossing rocks into the small river.

One evening, when it was time to go back to the school, I couldn't find my hoe. When Señorita Marielita found out, she got very upset. "If you can't find it," she scolded me, "you'll have to pay for it. Señorita Anita is going to be very angry."

I went to bed that night feeling very worried. The next morning, however, some of the other girls went with me to the little river, and we found my hoe under some rocks. I was so

relieved! Looking for my hoe was only a short diversion, however—we were soon back to work on the road. We were almost
halfway done and felt like experts in road construction. We
knew the width the road was to be, so at times we had to jump
on the ground to make it even. Finally, we finished the road—it
now reached Señorita Anita's house—and everyone started clap-
ping and jumping for joy. When we walked back to the grange
it seemed to me that it was very far away. I could hardly believe
that we had built a road by ourselves without anyone's help. We
did it by working together.

When Father Luna and Señorita Anita saw the road, they
could not believe that we had done great work all by ourselves.
They could now drive a truck to the little house that Señorita
Anita had received as a gift. Father Luna ordered a small shelter
to be built halfway between the grange and the little house, and
he placed a statue of the Virgin Mary there. He held a celebration there, where he held a mass and blessed the road.

As our reward for building the road, we were to get new uniforms. We could choose from two different colors—pink or
light green. We would wear these uniforms on Sundays and holidays. I asked for mine to be pink, which was my favorite color.
The first time we wore the uniforms was in May, the Virgin's
month, and we all looked very pretty.

When the new home was ready, Señorita Anita brought a
nun from Spain to be its director. Her name was Mother
Celina, and she was beautiful. She was very tall and slim, with
blue eyes and white skin. She wore a black habit, which made
her seem much taller. The first thing she did was to choose ten
girls from our grange to go to the new home with her—they
were to have a vocation as nuns and help Mother Celina start a
convent. The girls were excited, they moved to the new home,

and they got new white uniforms with a cloak that they could put over their heads. Although they came back to the grange every Sunday for mass, we noticed that their behavior had changed. They acted like they didn't know us; they didn't even say hello. I supposed that they had become quite serious about their apprenticeship and thought they were nuns already.

Mother Celina's girls were well behaved and serious, but some of the older girls at my little grange could still be unkind. I didn't have any kind of jewelry, but I admired a ring that belonged to one of the older girls. It was gold with an aquamarine stone—it was beautiful. The girl knew that I liked her ring, so one morning she proposed a deal: she said that if I gave her my bread for breakfast every day for five months in a row, she would give me her ring. I eagerly agreed, and I kept to my side of the bargain. I gave her my bread every single day, even though it hurt me to do it because I was hungry all morning. But we had made a deal, and she seemed very happy with her extra piece of bread each day.

Four months went by, and I became happier with each passing day, knowing that very soon I would have that ring on my finger. But one day, after the girl's mother had been to visit, I noticed that she wasn't wearing her ring.

"Where's your ring?" I asked.

"I don't have it anymore," she said, not seeming too concerned. "It actually belongs to my grandmother, and my mom wanted to return it to her."

I slapped her face hard. She started crying and told Señorita Marielita what I had done. Señorita Marielita called me over to her, and without even asking me if I had an explanation, she ordered me to kneel behind the bathroom, holding a brick in each hand. I was to stay there until she sent for me.

Time went by—lunch, recess, afternoon classes—and I continued holding the bricks. I got very tired and sat down, and I fell asleep for a short time. I woke up when I heard the girls using the bathroom, and I knelt down once more, holding the bricks in my hands. I was feeling very hungry, because I hadn't had lunch, and I supposed I had missed dinner as well: it was getting dark outside. Then I heard Señorita Marielita calling my name. She sounded frightened, and when she saw me, she hurried over to me and hugged me. She said that she had forgotten I was there. She kept hugging me and apologizing, asking me to forgive her. I understood that she hadn't intended for me to hold the bricks all day, but it would have been easier to forgive her if she hadn't taken my name off the Wall of Honor.

At this time, some of the older girls on the grange had started flirting with the older boys from the boys' grange. These boys looked after the cows and brought us our milk. They would come to the top of a hill almost every night; they brought lanterns, so we could tell they were there. They would play instruments and sing, as if they were serenading us. All the older girls really loved it. Once they finished singing, they would leave, and the girls would blow kisses to them. They would also exchange notes or letters with girls when they brought in the milk.

One night when we heard the boys playing their harmonicas, the older girls opened the window and lit matches, throwing them out into the air. This went on for about half an hour, and because they were giggling and talking, I couldn't fall sleep. I had just moved to place myself behind the girls, trying to get a better look, when all of a sudden Señorita Marielita stormed in and turned on the lights. She screamed, "Stop that this instant! The gas tanks are right under that window!"

The girls quickly apologized and handed Señorita Marielita the matches, but she was still furious. "Go to sleep," she said sternly. "You are going to be badly punished in the morning."

Everything got quiet, and I was very frightened. I wouldn't have been in trouble if I had stayed on my bed. I was going to be punished for being curious.

The next morning we all waited quietly for our punishment, but Señorita Marielita did not call us. After three days had gone by without word of our punishment, we thought that Señorita Marielita had forgotten all about it.

Then, on the fourth day, Señorita Anita came in just before bedtime and told us to go to the dining room. Once we had gathered there, she asked Señorita Marielita for the names of the girls who had misbehaved that night. We were all shaking with fear as we awaited our punishment.

"What you girls did is a very serious matter," Señorita Anita began. "You could have burned down the grange, and everyone could have died. For that reason, I must give you a very serious punishment." We nodded and held our breath, waiting to learn what the punishment would be. "I want you to go to the sewing room and get undressed."

We did as we were told, and when Señorita Anita joined us there a few minutes later, she told us to face the wall with our hands up in the air. She then asked her driver for his belt, which was made out of very thick leather. "I am going to whip each one of you," she said dispassionately, "and if you cry or scream, I will whip you more." She whipped our backs ten times each, hitting us without any compassion. I felt excruciating pain and was sure that I was going to die. Some of the girls fell down on the floor from the pain. Finally, she put down the belt. "From now on," she said, "I expect you to follow all the rules of the grange. Now, go take a shower with cold water and then go to sleep." With that, she left.

My back felt numb. When I looked at the other girls, I knew that my back looked as bad as theirs did—some had deep marks, very red, and some were bleeding. We were all shaking, and we started to cry as we stepped into the cold shower, which made our skin feel like it was burning. That night, I couldn't fall asleep. I had never seen Señorita Anita so severe or so out of control. I was scared to think that we had made her that angry.

A few weeks later, Señorita Anita sent us on a field trip. She stayed at the grange with the younger girls and sent the cook and Señorita Marielita with us. We brought our bathing suits, because she had told us there was a pool where we were going. We all climbed into the truck and sang songs, as we always did during field trips. Arriving at our destination, we saw that it was an estate with a huge house and lots of fruit trees, especially oranges. The owners said that we could eat as much fruit as we liked. The house belonged to friends of Señorita Anita. After eating some fruit, we played ball in a big field. Later, we had lunch and then went into the pool. The pool was deep, but had some spots where the younger girls could play. I wasn't afraid of the water, because I knew that Señorita Marielita wasn't going to let anybody push me under. Besides, I wasn't afraid of the older girls anymore. Señorita Marielita never went in the water, because she said that she didn't know how to swim, but she watched us as we played.

We were enjoying our time at the pool, when suddenly two of the girls who couldn't swim jumped into the deep end of the pool. A couple of the other girls tried to help them, but the frightened girls clutched at them and tried to pull them under. They were panicking in the deep water, so the would-be rescuers had to swim away or be drowned. Señorita Marielita started to take off her shoes to throw herself in the water, but some girls stopped her because she couldn't swim, either. Time seemed to stand still as the two girls fought for their lives. Finally, a few girls tied some clothes together to make a long rope and tossed it out to the girls struggling in the water. One of them grabbed onto it and was pulled safely out of the pool. But the other girl had stopped fighting; her hands weren't moving, and her hair was just floating in the water. Everyone screamed, and some girls went running for help but didn't find any. All of the sudden, we saw a young man running toward the pool. He dove in, grabbed the girl by her hair, and pulled her out of the water. When she was out, he placed her on her stomach and made her cough and spit up a lot of water. At first she seemed quite dazed, but after a while, she sat up on her own and seemed fine.

Señorita Marielita knelt down to kiss the young man's hands. "You are an angel!" she told him. "Thank you so much! I thank God that you were here."

"Thank God for that girl's long hair," he said. "Otherwise, I couldn't have pulled her out."

Later, when the girl was feeling better, we returned to the grange. Señorita Marielita said that she did not want to go on another field trip for a long time.

Now it was December, and we needed to practice Christmas carols. This Christmas, there were two teachers who decided to stay with us instead of going home for vacation; that made us very happy. They taught us new Christmas carols and wanted to have a *Posada*, a Christmas celebration that symbolizes the night when Mary and Joseph were looking for a place to stay. Nobody had a room for them, leaving them no choice but to stay in a stable full of farm animals.

For our Posada, we made about five small huts out of wood and branches, big enough to fit two or three people. We placed a little hut every thirty feet; and we all had to practice what we needed to say. One of the girls who was very pretty and had long hair dressed in white and played the part of the Virgin Mary. I was Joseph—I wore men's clothes and had a fake mustache. I wasn't sure I liked the idea of playing Joseph, but once I looked in the mirror I started laughing, and the rest of the girls joined me. The best part was that I got to guide a real donkey, with Mary sitting on top of it. We practiced and were ready for Christmas.

The teachers made *dulce de leche*, a caramel-like dessert, and a lot of pastries. They did not want to make tamales, because the process was too complicated, so we were to have ham, rice, and corn for our Christmas dinner. Señorita Anita wasn't able to join us but, as always, she sent lots of gifts and candy. This year, I was old enough to go with the older girls and place presents under the beds. We did this while the rest of the girls were playing on the basketball court.

We opened Señorita Anita's boxes, which were full of toys and clothes, and started placing the items on each girl's bed, first the clothes and pajamas, then the toys. Toys were chosen according to the age of the girl, and some were to receive beautiful dolls. When the time came for the teacher to put a toy on my bed, she hesitated and then asked, "Is it too childish to give you a doll?"

"Oh, no!" I responded happily. "I would very much like a doll."

She let me choose my doll, and I embraced it with love and placed it on my bed on top of my new clothes.

Once everything was set out on the beds, it was time to wrap the presents and place them underneath. We were all very tired by the time we finished. When we finally arrived downstairs, Father Agudelo had arrived to celebrate the midnight mass. As in other years, the boys from the boys' grange came to celebrate with us, as did Mother Celina and her novices. Everybody went to see the Christmas scene, which was very well illuminated and looked better than usual because the teachers had helped us to put it together.

We started the Posada, with the Virgin Mary sitting on her donkey and me, Saint Joseph, guiding it. Father Agudelo seemed very happy, and Mother Celina and her girls seemed to enjoy it too. After we finished the Posada, Father Agudelo started the holy Christmas mass, and we all sang and played our tambourines and maracas. That night, everything seemed enchanted. At the end of mass, Father Agudelo wished us a merry Christmas and blessed us all. Our neighbors were offered some of the sweets that the teachers had made, and they left very happy. As always, we all went to our rooms after dinner. When the girls saw the presents, they all squealed with delight. And another Christmas was over.

By this time I think I was about thirteen years old, but of course, I didn't know for certain. I just knew that I felt mature and wise. We continued with our classes, chores, and embroidery projects, which were getting better and better each day. One day Señorita Anita arrived when we were embroidering, and she looked very pleased to see the beauty of our work. On her next visit she brought us embroidery magazines full of new stitches for us to learn. She also brought some of her own blouses so we could make designs on them.

That spring, there was a period of time when it rained without stopping for five days. On one of those nights the rain and the lightning were so strong that we were afraid and went to pray in the chapel. We heard loud noises coming from the river that night, which made us even more afraid. The following day, a neighbor came to tell Señorita Marielita that the river had left its course three miles down the road and that many houses in the village had been washed away by the water. He said that some people had been killed. Very quickly, Señorita Marielita told us to collect some towels and sheets. She grabbed the first-aid box, and then we older girls went with her to the village.

We saw rocks and trees on the ground; the roads were muddy and full of pieces of wood from the houses that had been destroyed by the river. When we finally got to what was left of the village, we saw a horrible scene—the dead bodies of adults and two children lay on the ground before us. The scene made us cry. We could only pray for them and cover their bodies with our sheets. All of a sudden, we saw a young man in his late teens crying for his family. He knelt down by the bodies of the children, which were covered with mud and clay. Señorita Mariela told the young man that if he needed anything, all he needed to do was to go to Father Luna's Infant Grange and ask for help; the people there would be willing to help him in any way. We went back to the grange feeling very depressed. Señorita Marielita said that we were very lucky that our grange was located on top of a hill, because that protected it from the rushing river. Father Agudelo was unable to say mass for us that day. The roads were blocked with trees, and he couldn't get through to us. But we said a prayer on our own, thanking God that we were safe.

A couple of weeks later, Señorita Marielita told us to make sure the grange looked especially nice, because some American men were coming to make a movie about us. We were very excited.

The men arrived, bringing us presents and candy, and started directing us for the movie. They asked us to clear the dining room, as we did for Christmas, so there would be enough room to celebrate mass. Then we were sent to put on our Sunday uniforms. The men brought in about ten sewing machines, asking the older girls to sew—or, rather, to pretend to sew: none of us knew how. They started videotaping us, one of the men speaking in English as the rest worked the camera and other equipment. They asked us to cut and fold some fabric, as the older girls continued pretending to sew. The men stayed for a long time; they also videotaped the other rooms, the bedrooms, and the outdoor area of the grange, all the while speaking in English. When they were finished, they placed the sewing machines back in the truck and said good-bye to us. We were disappointed, because we thought they would let us keep some of the machines, but they just used them for the movie.

After the men had left, a teacher who spoke English translated what the narrator had said. He was thanking those who had sponsored their charitable work so that these schools could be built. The men presented us as children found on the streets—some of us as orphans, others as children in need of a comfortable place to call home, a place where we could receive a good education and learn to sew. The man kept repeating that thanks to the support from the donors, this school and schools like it had been built in these areas. When we heard this translation, some of us were offended—we had never lived on the streets. The teachers told us not to say anything to Señorita

Anita, because she didn't know anything about the film crew's visit: these men actually had nothing to do with Father Luna's grange. But the men were gone and their movie was made, and we didn't have anything to say about it.

Life went on as usual, until the Sunday morning when Mother Celina's novices came to visit us. "Mother's things are no longer in her room!" one of the girls said. "It looks like she left in the night, and we don't know where she is."

Señorita Marielita seemed very nervous. "I just can't believe that," she said, and neither could we. Soon afterward, the boys from the other school came over with a similar story—their director had disappeared! They all looked very sad and confused. It didn't take long for everyone to figure out that Mother Celina and the boys' director had gone off together. Father Agudelo came later on with the news that they had both left for Medellin, a large city in the nearby state of Antioquia.

By the next Sunday, Señorita Anita had already found a new director for the novices, but she wasn't a nun—she was a very well-educated and well-dressed young woman named Teresa. Apparently, Señorita Anita had said that she didn't want to know any more about nuns. Perhaps this nice young woman would stay longer than some of them had. Señorita Anita also brought us some tablecloths to embroider for the altar at the San Diego Church, Bogotá. She included threads of all colors, including gold. She wanted us to embroider grape branches around the border and a chalice in the center. All of these pictures were in the magazines that she brought for us, and she herself had chosen the pictures and threads. We were excited, and we began to embroider the cloths. When we finished a bunch of grapes, we all admired how beautiful it was, and then we continued. We wanted to finish it quickly to give to Señorita Anita, but it would take many weeks to finish.

When Señorita Anita returned, a few days later, she brought a small girl with her. She was about three years old, her name was Liza, and she was from a district called Choco, very far from the capital. We all ran to pick her up because she was so beautiful. Her skin was as dark as a black horse. I had never seen such a dark girl. Señorita Anita told us to take good care of her because she was very small and an orphan. I thought that she had come to a very good place, because she would be safe here. We all lost interest in the embroidery for a while, because we were watching Liza and wanting to be with her, talk to her, bathe her, brush her hair, and dress her. She seemed like a live doll. Señorita Marielita also watched her, of course, making sure that she ate and was happy.

Finally, though, we finished embroidering the cloths—the grapes looked real. We thought we would rest after that, but Señorita Marielita told us that we needed to embroider a tablecloth for the dining room so we could surprise Señorita Anita on her birthday. We only had one month for this project, so we embroidered every day after class and on Saturdays and Sundays.

Six of us girls were sewing in the dining room when Señorita Anita arrived to collect the tablecloths we had finished. We quickly hid her surprise and then gave her the cloths for the altar of the church of San Diego.

"Congratulations, girls," she said. "I can't believe how beautiful these are. Father Pena, my brother, who is the parish priest of the San Diego Church in Bogotá, will be very happy when he sees such beautiful work." She left very gratefully with the cloths.

As soon as she was gone, we began again on her birthday surprise. It didn't seem like we would have enough time to finish, so we embroidered until very late each night. When we finally completed our work, we started cheering for happiness. The cloth had turned out beautifully. Señorita Marielita hugged us and congratulated us on a beautiful job, then she wrapped it up in gift paper.

When Señorita Anita returned on her birthday, we sang to her and then presented her with her gift. When she opened it, she was as happy as I'd ever seen her. She loved our embroidery. We told her that it had been Señorita Marielita's idea, and so she thanked all of us.

10

Father Luna had the idea that our girls' grange should have a pool.

"I don't want anything to do with pools," Señorita Marielita said. "We had a bad experience, as you know."

"Well, that's just it, Señorita," Father Luna said logically. "If the girls know how to swim, they'll be much safer around the water. Almost all the boys' granges have pools. I've brought some men to get started on it."

Upon hearing this, we were all very happy—I wasn't afraid of water anymore.

And so it was that they started making a pool for us. The work lasted for several months, but finally it was ready. It was a medium-sized pool, and only five feet at its deepest. When the work was finished, Father Luna came and blessed the pool. From that day on, we enjoyed the water every day and learned to swim very quickly.

The year was about to end, and the teachers had left to spend Christmas with their families. We stayed at the grange with Señorita Marielita, who promised us that she would not leave for any more vacations—she still remembered her last trip away, and poor Olivia's experience and her burned hands. Christmas arrived, and everything was much the same as in past years—the mass, the dinner, the presents. I remembered how excited I'd been on my first Christmas at the grange, and now, although I still looked forward to it, it would never be quite as special as when I was little. According to Señorita Anita's records, I was fourteen years old; I was developing and becoming a young woman.

It already worried me that I would have to leave when I turned eighteen. I didn't know anything about my family's whereabouts. I didn't even know if they were still alive. I was afraid of life outside of the grange; I didn't know what life would be like in the outside world.

After the Christmas and New Year's celebrations, Señorita Anita sent for me. She hugged me and said, "Maria Luisa, I have good news. A college in Bogotá has given me scholarships for three girls—and you're one of them. You are very intelligent, and you'll do well."

When I heard this, I didn't know whether to be happy or sad. "Señorita," I began slowly, "I'm very grateful, but I don't know if I want to leave the grange."

"Of course you must go," she said. "You'll be happy there, and I know you'll enjoy studying." She patted my arm and smiled. "I'll come back for you and the other two girls next week. You'll need to have all your belongings ready."

Señorita Anita left, and I knew that my life—which had been so steady and consistent for all these years—was about to change.

I started packing right away. I looked at my doll, and as I held it tightly in my arms, I decided right then to give it to Liza. I told her it was a gift to remember me by, and I asked her to take good care of it.

Time went by quickly, and after a week, Señorita Anita came back in a rush.

"Maria Luisa, is there another hardworking and responsible girl who would benefit from a scholarship?"

Without hesitation, I said, "Yes, Señorita. Rosa is good; Rosa even prays during recess time."

"Then go find her," Señorita Anita said, "and tell her to gather her belongings as quickly as possible."

I did not see Señorita Marielita anywhere, but I didn't have to go far to find Rosa. When I told her, she ran very quickly to pack her things. And so, after saying our good-byes, we left my little grange and began the trip to the capital. I had expected to feel sad about leaving, but I was too excited to be starting my new adventure. Besides, I had friends with me this time. Inside the bus, Luz and Maruja—the two girls who had been chosen with me originally—were wondering why Rosa was with us.

"Señorita Anita had an extra scholarship," I explained, "and she decided to give it to Rosa."

When we arrived in Bogotá, we were taken to a huge house. It was already late, but even in the dark I remembered that I had been brought to this house seven years ago, on my way to the grange. Señorita Anita told us that we were to stay in that house for the night and that she would return for us the following day.

The couple who lived there now—not the same couple from my first visit—prepared something for us to eat, and the women asked us many questions about our grange and where we were going. I told her all the beautiful things I knew about the grange where I had lived for seven years.

I hardly slept that night. It suddenly occurred to me that if my family finally visited me at the grange, I would not be there anymore. But maybe they had already forgotten about me. I thought about how big my brothers must be now. All I wanted was for my family to know that I was fine, happy, and healthy, and that I was going to study in Bogotá.

Señorita Anita came for us in the morning, and we left for the school. Once we got there, the Mother Superior talked with Señorita Anita for a while, and then Señorita Anita said good-bye to us, promising that she and Father Luna would each visit us once a month.

Then the Mother Superior introduced us to a nun named Cecilia, who was to be in charge of us. "If you have any questions," she said, "Madre Cecilia is the right person to talk to." Then she took us to our bedroom. It was enormous: there were six beds, and two girls were already in the room. Then Madre Cecilia, as we were to call her, gave us a tour of the school. It had six floors, and I think it must have taken up the whole block; it even had a nursing home on the first floor. Its staircases were very wide, with a lot of plants on them. Its floors were made of marble, and the hallways were very large. A few university students who studied elsewhere lived there, as did a number of young women who worked outside of the school. They lived in other sections of the building. It felt like a dream to be in such a beautiful, grand place. We went to eat lunch, and the dining room was so spacious that it was divided into sections. In our section, there were thirty teenage girls. The nuns served us, and they were attentive to the girls. A nun read to us while we ate, and we all listened quietly. After lunch, we left the plates on the table and headed into a large yard with a basketball court and other games. There, we spoke with the other girls and began making friends. Later, everyone went to their classes. After classes, everyone went to pray and eat dinner. After dinner, we could choose to go to recess or to our room to do our homework before going to sleep.

The next day—and each day after that—we woke up at 6:30 in the morning. After bathing ourselves, we got in line to go to mass. After mass, we went to eat breakfast and then to our classes.

The next day a nun took our measurements to make us our uniforms. Our everyday uniforms were a light blue color; the uniforms for special occasions were dark blue. Both had white collars and sleeves. We also wore black shoes and white stockings.

My uniforms fit me perfectly, and I liked the way they looked. But Madre Cecilia warned us to be very careful and not to stain them. For me, this was easy: I was used to taking care of my uniforms at the grange.

After the first few weeks, I had become used to the routine and rules of my new school. I missed the grange, though, and I missed Señorita Marielita and the girls. Even though this school was very elegant and modern, I preferred living on the grange.

Señorita Anita came to visit us, as promised, and we were happy to see her. We would have loved to sing to her like we did at the grange, but this place was very different.

"Madre Cecilia has spoken very well of you girls," Señorita Anita said. "She says that you are behaving yourselves and that she is very pleased with you. Now tell me: How are your studies going? Are you happy?"

I spoke up first. "Yes, Señorita. We are very happy, but I miss Señorita Marielita and the girls."

Señorita Anita hugged me. "You should write them a letter, and I will take it to them." I thought that was a very good idea.

Father Luna came to visit about a week later; he was a good friend of the Mother Superior, and after speaking with her, he called us to him one by one. When it was my turn, the first thing that I did was to kneel down and ask for his blessing. Then, he told me to come and sit beside him. I was nervous, because I had never talked with him in private before. He put his hand on my shoulder and gave me a lot of caring advice, and when he was finished, he ran his hand over my cheek and told me to keep behaving myself so that the grange's name would be respected.

I continued with my studies, and I had no problems learning; I was even starting to like mathematics, because the Mother who taught the class had a lot of patience and took a lot of time to explain things to me. We also had singing classes, and they taught us a lot of new songs. What surprised me most was that they didn't punish us and hardly ever scolded us—or maybe that was only because we followed the rules.

We went to mass every day, and twice on Sundays. The nuns sang very beautifully, accompanied by organ or piano. It was a very big church, and it was always full of people, especially on Sundays and holidays.

After we had been at the school for a few months, Madre Cecilia informed us that there were dressmaking classes on Saturdays, and that if we were interested, we could learn to sew. I liked embroidery and cross-stitch a lot, so I promised Madre Cecilia that I wouldn't miss a class. When Señorita Anita returned to visit us, I asked if she would please bring me some material: I was really excited about dressmaking.

"This is what I want to hear from you, Maria," she said. "That you are learning and learning!"

The sewing teacher was a woman who came from outside the school. She was very elegant and pretty, and she dressed very well. When she gave me my notebook, I put my name on the inside cover: "Maria Luisa Morales, Dressmaking Notebook." I could hardly believe that I would learn to make dresses and sew. When Señorita Anita returned, she brought me some very beautiful material. She also brought a new dress that was too big for me. "Use your imagination, Maria," she instructed. "Take it apart and use the material to make a dress for yourself." The fabric was lovely; it had tiny violets and roses, in beautiful colors. I made the huge dress into one that fit me, and I wore it for the first time that Sunday. After mass on Sundays, we could wear our own clothing if we wanted to.

I was really happy with my dressmaking classes, because the teacher had already taught me how to sew with the machine. My stitches were very straight, and I already knew how to make my own patterns and take measurements. I was learning a lot in these classes.

Almost all the girls at the new school had relatives who visited them, and sometimes they took them away for weekends. Because I didn't have anyone, I stayed at school, practicing sewing and reading. Father Luna visited us often, and when it was my turn to speak with him, he sat very close to me and hugged me. He always gave me advice and offered very kind words. I always paid close attention to him, but sometimes he came so close to me that I got nervous. He always said good-bye by touching my cheek and running his hand over my jaw; he also always gave me a coin, for which I was very grateful because I could use the money to buy sweets and sodas.

Time flew by, and it was almost the end of the year—time for final exams. I started to think about where I would be sent after this year. I wondered if I would have to return to the grange. According to my records, I was fifteen years old, and I felt very grown up.

Everything went well with my exams, and Señorita Anita was very happy with me. She told me and the other girls that we could stay at the school during vacation if we helped the nuns with their chores—watering the plants, cleaning the floors, and helping with the old women. Rosa and I decided to stay. We helped the nuns every day, but they gave us a lot of freedom, too.

Some of the nuns asked me why I didn't leave to be with my family for vacation, and I told them that they lived very far away and couldn't come for me. I thought about Tia Trinita; eight years had gone by, and I had never heard anything from her. Maybe it was for the best that my aunt Trinita had sent me to Father Luna's Infant Grange. If she hadn't, I would probably still be out in the countryside, without an education and living in fear of the guerrillas. Instead, I was safe at a home where I was learning many things, and I was going to school in Bogotá. I thanked God for my good fortune.

When I had been at the school for almost a year, I realized that there were still places that I hadn't discovered yet, because the school was so big. I had recently discovered a room in the back of the school where the nuns played music on Sundays. Some of the older girls sometimes joined them. There was also a television there—this was exciting for me, the first time I had actually seen a TV. I was delighted to have discovered this room; I now knew where to go on Sundays to listen to music and spend time with the other girls.

I was glad to have made new friends, because I didn't see much of Rosa anymore. She no longer shared a room with us, because she had become a novice. I saw her at church, but I couldn't talk to her, so little by little I lost her friendship. I cared about her, though: she was a very good person.

Christmas at the college was very different from our celebration at the grange. At this college, the nuns did everything. They made the Nativity in the church, close to the altar, and we couldn't get too close to it or take part in creating it. They celebrated the Christmas mass at midnight, and many people came. The church was filled with them, and the nuns sang beautifully, as if they were angels. But there was no special dinner and no gifts under our beds. I really missed my grange at Christmas.

A few days later, Señorita Anita came to visit me. She wished me a merry Christmas and gave me some gifts—boxes of clothes and two pairs of fine shoes. She told me that one of the pairs of shoes belonged to Father Luna but were too small for him. They looked brand new and were very fine shoes. I took them and wore them on Sundays after mass. Many of the girls laughed at me because they were men's shoes, but I didn't care. I kept wearing them.

"Thank you very much, Señorita," I said. "I miss the way we celebrated Christmas at the grange."

Señorita Anita smiled and hugged me. "Things change, Maria Luisa. We miss having you there, but you're growing up now. And good news—the nuns have said you may stay here for another year."

Classes started up again after the Christmas season. I realized that the other girls from my grange weren't back this year, and I never saw them again. Little by little, I lost contact with them all. Still, Father Luna visited me often. He always brought me to the same private place, and he always sat very close to me. He would hug me and give me his advice; then he would take my hands in his and kiss them, saying very sweet words. I felt uncomfortable—I didn't think this was right for a priest to do.

After his visits, though, I would forget all about it. I continued my studies, and I was learning more and more. I began a nursing class and learned about first aid and how to give injections.

Señorita Anita hadn't been to visit me for a few months, and I was getting worried that I would not see her again. Then, finally, she came to see me.

"Maria Luisa, I want you to learn more dressmaking this year, because at the end of the year, I am going to bring you back to your grange. You are to help me teach the girls to sew and help Señorita Marielita with the little ones."

My eyes widened in surprise—this was a big responsibility. "Yes, Señorita Anita," I said. "I will do what you say!"

Because I was now living in the capital city, political unrest was a fact of life. For a few months, there were a lot of disturbances near the president's palace, and we could hear gunshots at night. Many people were killed, and the nuns sent us to bed very early to protect us. On one of those nights, one of the girls who lived at our school was killed. She studied at a university outside of the school, but she had lived with us. We held a vigil for her in the school's church, and everyone was extremely sad.

Eventually, I became great friends with two girls named Blanca and Gladys. They were a little older than me, and we always went to the special room together to listen to music on Sundays. We took walks outside, sometimes around the school and sometimes to the national park. There were a lot of people there, many with children. One day, the three of us were sitting on the grass at the park, eating some sweets and chatting. When it was time for us to go back to the school, we realized that our purses were missing. Thieves had stolen our things as we sat talking, and we'd never heard them. Although it was annoying, it wasn't as bad as it could have been—none of us had any money. Our purses were filled with silly things like handkerchiefs and combs. We thought the joke was on the thieves!

Everything was going well for me in my classes, and my teachers always spoke well of me. I did especially well in my dressmaking class, and I was well aware of it. I already knew how to make my own dresses. In my notebook, I had written all the instructions I needed for taking measurements, cutting materials, making skirts, and cutting and putting together collars.

Final exams arrived, and I was very nervous—as I was every year. But I passed my grade, and now I just had to wait for Señorita Anita to come for me. I was thinking about this when Madre Cecilia told me to get my things ready because Señorita Anita would be coming for me the next day. I spent that evening saying good-bye to the nuns and the other girls, but I didn't get a chance to say good-bye to Rosa. This hurt a lot, because we had been good friends.

The next day, Señorita Anita sent the driver to pick me up and bring me to the huge house where I had stayed two years earlier. After a few hours, Father Luna arrived, and the women who lived in the house knelt down to greet him and ask for his blessing. Then he told one of the women that he wanted to talk with me. He brought me to a private room, and he offered very caring words as he took my hands between his and kissed them. I simply stayed quiet. I knew, even as young as I was, that this affection was not appropriate.

The next day, Señorita Anita came for me and we headed back to the grange. She said that she was going to pay me for teaching the girls to sew and helping Señorita Marielita. I was about sixteen years old, but I couldn't study anymore. I was needed to help the girls. When we arrived, all the girls greeted

Señorita Anita and sang to her, as they always did. Señorita Marielita hugged me, and the other girls who knew me also ran up to greet me.

"I'm so happy that you're going to be my assistant," Señorita Marielita told me. Then Señorita Anita told all the girls that she had brought me there so that I could help Señorita Marielita to take care of them. "You must respect and obey Maria Luisa," Señorita Anita said. "She is going to teach you to sew. She is an exemplary young woman, who is full of ideas."

I blushed, hearing so much praise of myself. When Señorita Anita left, Señorita Marielita brought me to my room, which had been Señorita Maruja's room some years ago. I couldn't believe that I would have my own room now—how different everything would be!

Although I was glad to be back at my little grange, I wasn't very excited about my job. I would've liked to continue studying in Bogotá, but I had no choice. Right away, I started to teach the girls what I knew about sewing. There were two new sewing machines for the girls, and there was also a lot of material to make dresses. It seemed that I was going to be very busy with sewing. I also taught them a lot of the songs that I had learned at school in the capital. Not everything went smoothly with my new job. Sometimes the bigger girls rebelled against me because they were older and didn't want me to teach them. I was to eat in the director's and teachers' dining room, because I was on the same level as them, but I wasn't happy about that. I would have preferred to eat with the girls. The only thing that I enjoyed was the pool; we went swimming every day after lunch. Even Señorita Marielita went swimming now!

Christmas was coming, and we started making the Nativity scene and practicing the carols. One afternoon, while we were practicing, Father Luna came to visit. After speaking with Señorita Marielita for a while, he sent for me. The meeting was in his room. He closed the door after I entered, and we sat on a small sofa.

"I really came just to see you, Maria," he said, "because I miss you a lot on those days when I don't see you. Are you happy here at the grange?"

"Yes, Father, I am," I answered quickly, but I don't think he was listening to me—he was looking at my breasts and kissing my hands.

He told me sweet words that no one had ever told me, and then I felt his lips on my cheek and his hands on my breasts. The cologne he had on was so strong. I felt a million feelings, including fear, all at the same time. I couldn't believe this was happening to me. Then he got very nervous and stood up quickly. "You may go," he whispered.

Señorita Marielita met me as I was coming out of the room. "Have you done confession with Father Luna?"

"Yes, Señorita, I confessed, and he gave me a lot of advice." I felt very bad for lying, but I couldn't tell her the truth. Last year, I was thinking that I was finally protected and that I was no longer in danger of being sexually molested. But now, I realized that there was no safe place.

It was the day before Christmas, and I was involved in everything because I had to help Señorita Marielita with it all—especially so on this day, because Señorita Marielita had a horrible headache. The biggest girls were helping with the boxes, and we started to separate the clothes by size and put them on the girls' beds. By the time we finished the Christmas night routine, Señorita Marielita was feeling better. The priest who was going to do the mass arrived—it wasn't Father Agudelo now; it was a new priest, a kind young man. I enjoyed the familiarity of my grange Christmas—the novices came to celebrate, and the boys from the grange. When it was time to go to sleep, Señorita Marielita handed me an envelope. I opened it and found money, which Señorita Anita had sent me for Christmas. I was very happy, because I had never had so much money in my hands. I fell asleep thinking about how much I could buy for myself. It was a happy Christmas.

After the Christmas season was over, we had to clean out all of the classrooms to get everything ready for the new classes. Señorita Anita arrived and said she would be spending a few days with us. It was a busy time.

One night, as I was talking with Señorita Marielita, I noticed that she seemed a little distracted.

"You seem really tired, Señorita," I said. "Why don't you go to bed? I can finish whatever needs to be done."

"Thank you, Maria Luisa. I think I will."

After putting everything in order, I went to sleep, too. I slept soundly, but when I awoke the next morning, I realized that I hadn't heard Señorita Marielita ring the bell to wake up the girls, so I got up and went to her room to get her. I knocked very lightly, and she didn't answer. I knocked louder, but I still didn't hear anything. I opened the door a crack, and started in alarm. Señorita Marielita was having convulsions. Her face was almost purple, and her eyes were bulging out.

I ran to tell Señorita Anita. I knocked loudly on her door, calling out, "Something horrible is happening to Señorita Marielita!"

Señorita Anita jumped from her bed and ran to Señorita Marielita's room. "Call all the boys' granges until you find my driver!" she said wildly. "Tell him to come immediately with the director and other men! Quickly! This is an emergency!"

After doing this, I called to Julia, the cook, who ran back to Señorita Marielita's room with me. Señorita Anita was getting her dressed, and she told me to find something to hold her tongue because it was going down her throat and choking her. After that, I gathered the girls together and explained to them that Señorita Marielita was very ill. We were all very afraid. Soon, the driver came with the director of the boys' grange. They carried Señorita Marielita out on a stretcher and put her in the truck to travel to Facatativa, where there was a good hospital.

The girls, Julia, and I stayed there by ourselves at the grange. We didn't know what would happen to Señorita Marielita. I was extremely worried, not just for Señorita Marielita, but also because now there was no director. I couldn't replace her—I was just a girl. The director of the other girls' grange came to stay with us, for which I was very grateful. At dusk, Señorita Anita arrived and very sadly told us that Señorita Marielita had suffered a stroke. Her condition was very critical; if she recovered, she would be paralyzed. This made us even sadder, and we cried a lot. I loved Señorita Marielita like I loved my aunt Trinita.

The next day, when Señorita Anita returned from the hospital, she gave us the horrible news that Señorita Marielita had died of a brain hemorrhage. We all cried relentlessly, incapable of believing what had happened. We had lost our wonderful director, who was like a mother to us. The grange was filled with the sound of sobbing.

Señorita Anita sent for two directors from other granges, Alicia and Maritza, to give us advice and help us through this time of great suffering.

Señorita Anita said that all the girls needed to go to the funeral, and we boarded two trucks and headed to the town of Facatativá. Once we were there, we entered the church and saw the coffin with Señorita Marielita's body. After the ceremony, we walked past her coffin, one by one, to say good-bye one last time. From there, the body was carried to the cemetery. Then we returned to our grange, and Señorita Anita spoke with the new directors.

"I would like Maria Luisa to continue teaching the girls to sew," she said. "I am going to bring in a new director to take Señorita Marielita's place."

Then Señorita Maritza spoke up. "I would like to stay here as the director, Señorita. I promise to be the best director I can. I also have a niece who has graduated with a degree in dressmaking and who has a lot of teaching experience."

Señorita Anita looked pensive. "I will think about it. In the meantime, I would like you and Alicia to take care of the girls."

11

The teachers came back from their vacations a few days later, greatly saddened by Señorita Marielita's death. Señorita Maritza's niece, the dressmaking teacher, arrived as well. Señorita Alicia, sensing that I might not be needed here, suggested that I return with her to the San Francisco grange. "It's a boys' grange, but it also has a place for people on vacation to stay. You could serve tables or wash dishes or make beds. Or you could mend and sew the boys' clothes. I can pay you more than you're getting now. You would do very well."

"That's a lot to think about," I responded. "When Señorita Anita comes back, I'll tell her about this."

Señorita Anita returned shortly after that, and the directors spoke with her in private. Then she sent for me. "If this is really what you want, it's fine with me. I only want you to be happy."

"It's Señorita Alicia who wants to take me," I explained.

"Well, the decision has already been made. You'll be going to San Francisco with Señorita Alicia."

"Would it be possible," I ventured, "for me to keep studying with the other girls? I really want to study for at least two more years."

"I'm sorry, Maria, but I've already made my decision. I've also decided that Señorita Maritza will remain as the new director, and her niece will be the assistant and dressmaking teacher."

How quickly she had decided my life for me! Maybe it would have been different if I had my family nearby—they would have had to give permission before I was sent to a new place. But I had no one to speak for me. The next day, the truck came to take us on the four-hour trip to the San Francisco grange. This grange had about fifty boys, one director, three teachers, two cooks, and three young girls. I was to share a room with Señorita Alicia. After I arranged my things in my room, one of the young girls gave me a tour. I only saw part of the grange, because it was so big, but what I did see was very nice. There were many fruit trees and some farm animals—pigs, chickens, ducks, and cattle. A large river ran along the edge of the property. The first floor of the building was for all the boys, with a separate kitchen, classrooms, and bedrooms. The second floor had another kitchen and the director's rooms. The bedroom I shared with Señorita Alicia and the other girls' bedrooms were on this floor, as were the cooks' rooms.

The third floor was for vacationers; there were about ten really large bedrooms and a few bathrooms. There was also a rather large chapel where they held holy mass on special occasions. A lot of people came from Bogotá to spend their vacations there. The house was accented with many beautiful plants, and one of my jobs was to water them and keep them in good condition. That first night, I went to sleep very tired. I could have slept very late the next day, but we had to get up at about four o'clock in the morning in order to make the bread for breakfast. I was shown how to put the flour on a large platter, then add yeast, some eggs, and water, and mix it until it formed dough. I kneaded it until it took on a soft texture, and then I covered it and let it rise for two hours. The next step was to take a bit of dough in my hands and roll it into a ball. Some of the other girls had a lot of practice and were able to do so very quickly. In only a few minutes, they had many trays of bread. I watched in awe, but they laughed and told me that in a few months I would be a professional like them. Some of the older boys turned on the oven, which was located outside at the back of the kitchen. The brick oven was huge, about eight feet by six feet. When the oven was hot enough, they put in the bread—they had to be very careful, because the bread could burn easily.

All of this was a very rapid but delicate process. By about eight in the morning, the vacationers began to come down to eat their breakfast. The other girls made fresh orange juice for them and served them quickly; the vacationers wanted to eat right away. Señorita Alicia told me to pay very close attention, because this was going to be my daily job. After breakfast, I washed the plates and cleaned off the tables in the dining room, then I went outside to water the plants. I then ate a quick breakfast of my own before going upstairs to make the beds and clean the bedrooms. Next, I mended the boys' clothes—and this was all before lunch! When lunchtime arrived, we served the vacationers again. We had to make sure that they were happy with their meals, because our next summer's business depended upon their satisfaction.

After lunch we washed the dishes and cleaned the tables once more. We also had to mop the floors. Then, we continued mending the children's clothes until dinner, when we repeated the lunch routine. I finished that day extremely tired and slept soundly until four in the morning, when it was time to make the bread and start the routine all over again. Every day was much the same as the previous one. Then one day a car arrived after lunch, and everyone went to greet Father Luna. I had been so busy that I had not given any thought to him for weeks. He emerged from his car, blessing everyone there, but I could see that he was scanning the crowd for me. I looked at the ground, because it embarrassed me to look him in the eyes. We all went back to our chores when he started talking with the boys' director. He went up to his room after their meeting, and not even five minutes after that, the director told me that Father Luna wanted to talk to me. "It seems," the director said, "that Father Luna does not agree that you should be working here. He feels you are too young."

I didn't know what to say, so I just nodded to the director and started walking toward Father Luna's room. He met me on the staircase—as if, afraid I wouldn't answer his summons, he had come to find me—and ushered me into his room. He shut the door, saying his usual sweet words. "You are so lovely, Maria Luisa. I don't want you working here."

"This is what Señorita Anita wanted," I responded.

He shook his head as he moved closer to me and began stroking my arms. "I am trying to convince her to bring you back to the girls' grange." His hands moved all over my body, and this time he opened my blouse and took off my bra. I stood there, frozen, not knowing what to do. He stared at my naked chest and then began kissing my breasts, over and over again. I tried to cover myself up, but he stopped me. "Do not be afraid," he whispered as he continued kissing me. "All of this is very normal." Once again I smelled his strong cologne, and his kisses burned my face. When he finally went into the bathroom, I quickly left the room and returned to my chores.

I knew that what Father Luna was doing was wrong, but how could I refuse him? Everyone feared and respected him. I was mending the boys' clothes and thinking about this problem when I smelled his cologne again and heard the door close behind him. He took a bottle of perfume from his pocket and handed it to me. "Remember me," he said very kindly, "whenever you wear this perfume." Then he left for his home in Bogotá once more.

Father Luna never warned me not to tell anyone about what he was doing. Maybe he thought no one would believe me, or maybe he thought my loyalty to him was strong enough to buy my silence. Whatever the reason, I kept his actions to myself. I was very shy and incapable of confessing a secret like that.

On the weekends everything was the same as during the week, except that we had to get up even earlier than usual—we had to make bread for the priest and his family. Señorita Alicia made a few loaves of special bread with marmalade inside and a few more filled with cheese, then she packed them all in white linen. It all looked delicious, and it reminded me of when I was very small and my aunts and grandmother had baked for the priest. At seven in the morning, we girls, Señorita Alicia, the boys, and the director all went to the eight o'clock mass. The church in San Francisco was large and impressive. The boys from the grange sang very beautifully at the mass, and the church was filled with people.

One of my other tasks was to clean a house near the grange, a spacious place that the vacationers used. Because we had no car, we had to carry all our cleaning supplies and fresh linens. One morning, as I was coming down the path with a cumbersome load in my arms, a man stepped into my path. "What's a pretty girl like you doing carrying all those heavy things?" he said teasingly. I just stared at him, and he laughed. "Don't you remember me?"

I shook my head, wishing he would move out of my way.

"My name's Tito. I helped to make the pool at the girls' grange in Alban. I remember seeing you there." I looked at him more closely, and then I did remember him. He was a very handsome young man—tall, very pale, with a kind face. "My parents live nearby; I've come to visit them." We talked for a while longer, and then he asked if we could meet there the next day. I said yes.

I did all my chores quickly the next morning: I wanted to get down to the path and meet up with Tito. His face broke into a smile as he saw me hurrying toward him.

"I brought you some chocolates," he said. "I'm glad you came."

"Thank you," I said shyly.

"I'm going to be staying with my family for another month. After that, I'm going to join the army, but I want to keep seeing you before I have to go."

I felt myself blushing as he told me this. Then he took my hand and kissed it, and I felt my heart flutter. This was a really special young man.

"I … I have to go now," I stammered.

"Can we see each other in mass on Sunday?"

I nodded and then quickly turned and ran down the path to the big house.

That Sunday, Tito was in the church when I arrived with the other girls. He greeted me by nodding in my direction, and he kept watching me. When mass ended, he came over to me to say hello. Some of the girls recognized him, because he passed by the grange every now and then, but none of them knew his name.

"Would you like to have coffee with me, Maria?"

I grinned at him. "Wait just one minute while I ask Señorita Alicia's permission."

Señorita Alicia pursed her lips. "Where did you meet this young man?"

"His family lives near here," I explained. And I reminded her that he had helped build our pool.

She thought about it for a minute and then said, "Very well, Maria. You may go—but two of the other girls must accompany you."

And so it was that the four of us went out for coffee. Tito was very kind to me—and to the other girls, too, although he really only looked at me. After breakfast, he accompanied us back to the grange and said good-bye to everyone. Then, in a low voice, he said, "I will be waiting for you tomorrow, as always."

"I'll be there," I promised.

The other girls started to tease me. "Look at this innocent little one—who already has an admirer," one said. They laughed a lot, but I knew it was friendly teasing.

I continued with my daily chores. The work was so hard that I began to lose a lot of weight. Still, I was growing accustomed to such labor.

The day of Tito's departure quickly arrived. On the night before he was to leave, we met at dusk on the lower part of the path to the big house. I was nervous and sad, because I didn't know when I would see him again. Because it was getting dark, I didn't see him at first. I was afraid he had decided not to meet me. Just as I was about to go back to the grange, I felt someone grab my shoulder. I was frightened for a moment, then I saw that it was Tito; he had jumped the fence. We sat down on the dirt path, and he hugged me and cuddled with me. When he kissed me on the lips, I really felt that I loved him. I had never felt so much love in my heart. He told me that he loved me, and he promised to write to me soon.

I couldn't stay long, because I was afraid that someone would discover that I was gone. He walked with me almost to the grange's gate, and then said good-bye, promising again to write to me.

When I went in, the girls looked at me in surprise.

"Oh, Maria," one said nervously. "When we couldn't find you, we went to the chapel to tell Señorita Alicia that you were missing!"

I felt the blood drain from my face. "What ... what did she say?"

"Nothing," the girl answered. "She just kept praying. But I know she heard me."

Soon after, Señorita Alicia called me to her room. She looked at me sternly. "I know that you have been seeing that young man," she said coldly. "I know that you met with him tonight. But that was the last time. I'm going to have to tell Señorita Anita about your inappropriate behavior."

"But Señorita," I tried to explain, "he's leaving for the army. I just wanted to say good-bye to him."

Her face seemed to soften, and she hugged me. "All right, Maria. Just remember that everything I tell you is for your own good. The next time you have an admirer, speak with me first. Men often take advantage of young girls like you who have no family nearby."

I was thinking to myself that perhaps she should be having this talk with Father Luna. Maybe he had been fresh with me because he saw me as being alone, with no family.

Señorita Anita visited us every month to get the money obtained from the vacationers and pay us our salaries. I was happy with my salary, and I was able to save some money. I received letters from Tito, although Señorita Alicia always read them before passing them on to me. I thanked God that his letters were always sweet and respectful.

Most of the time I has very content with my life, although I was a little tired from time to time because of the hard work. According to my calculation, I was seventeen years old. I noticed that the older boys and some of the male teachers had begun to look at me admiringly. I was increasingly uncomfortable, though, with Father Luna's behavior. He would visit twice a month, and he continued to "play his games" with me. I began to get a stomachache whenever he called me into his room, as I was becoming more and more afraid of what he might do.

One day a visitor arrived with a parrot. It was a beautiful animal with blue, red, green, and yellow feathers, and a tail two feet long. The visitor gave it to Señorita Alicia as a gift, but Señorita Alicia did not like birds and let us take care of it. The parrot's name was Lulu, and she would walk through the hallways as if she were a puppy. But after she did this, I was responsible for picking up her mess. One of the men made a cage for Lulu and then placed it in the laundry room, because that was where I spent most of my time.

Lulu would climb to my shoulder and tickle me on my neck, head, and behind my ears. She would try to reach my mouth to touch my teeth and tongue. She would pick through my hair with her beak and say "piojito," *lice,* and "give me your leg," which made everyone laugh.

I left her in her cage in the laundry room at night, and she was usually a good bird. But one evening I left her cage open, and she got out. She perched herself on the laundry line, where all the professors' shirts were left to dry, and she ate all the buttons off them! That morning, when we got up to bake the bread, I heard Lulu squawking "Give me your leg" and ran to check on her. I found her perched, quite happily, on the buttonless shirts. Señorita Alicia was quite angry about this, and she told me that I needed to buy new buttons and fix all the shirts. At least she didn't tell me that I needed to get rid of Lulu!

One morning, three of us were baking the bread when the earth started to shake. The bread trays rattled, and the lamp on the ceiling started to swing from side to side. Everyone ran out to the patio on the first floor. Señorita Alicia rushed downstairs, too, and saw some older boys running out of the room below the bakery. They were not supposed to be there—that was where we kept the grains, corn, and beans—but she did not question them at that point. We were all too concerned about the earthquake. We were so scared that we were shaking almost as much as the ground.

"Let's wait outside a little longer," Señorita Alicia suggested. "I've heard that after an earthquake, there's usually another, smaller one." There was, but we were expecting this one, and it wasn't so scary. When it was safe, we all went back to our daily routine. And that's when Señorita Alicia asked the boys why they had been in the grain room. Finally, sheepishly, they confessed that they sometimes went in that room because they could see through the slats in the bakery's wooden floor. If they waited quietly, they could see the legs of the girls who were baking the bread. After that, Señorita Alicia had the floor in the bakery covered. Who knows how many times those boys got to see her legs, too?

Christmas came again, and we did not have vacationers with us. We had some free time to go shopping or to visit relatives.

Everything was different here. We did not have a Nativity scene, although we did sing Christmas carols. We decorated the chapel with flowers, and Father Luna came on Christmas Eve to hear our confessions. I did not want to have confession with him. I thought it would be better if I had another priest, but Father Luna was the only one there. At mass that night, everybody but me received communion from him—I could not bring myself to do so. Father Luna had spoiled my concept of a priest. Now that he was molesting me, I felt betrayed.

That following spring I became very ill. Most of the time I was very thirsty and tired, and the only thing I wanted to eat was fruit. I grew more tired each day. Señorita Alicia noticed my symptoms and told the other girls that I was pregnant. She called Señorita Anita, who came right away and ushered me into a room. She sat me in a chair and stood over me, looking quite fierce.

"With whom did you have sexual intercourse, Maria Luisa? Who is the father of your baby?"

I was quite frightened and could barely speak. Finally, I asked, "Could I get pregnant from being kissed?"

Señorita Anita slapped me on the face. "Don't play dumb with me! Tell me the truth!"

I swallowed hard, wondering if I could actually be pregnant. "A boy kissed me a few times, but that's all." I did not tell her that Father Luna kissed me and touched me.

She then called Señorita Alicia, who was also very nervous. "What has gone on here, Alicia?" Señorita Anita demanded.

Señorita Alicia sighed. "There was a boy who used to live nearby. He was interested in Maria, but he was sent to the army. I know he writes letters to her, but that's all I know."

I was listening to their conversation, even though I was beginning to feel worse and worse. Suddenly, I vomited on the floor in front of them.

"Well, that confirms it!" Señorita Anita snapped. "She's pregnant."

Señorita Anita seemed quite upset, and when she left a few minutes later, she told Señorita Alicia to keep her informed about my condition.

All the girls "knew" I was pregnant—at least, that's what Señorita Anita had told them. They asked me how I had gotten myself into such a mess. I truly didn't know. I felt increasingly sick for the next three weeks, and I had lost so much weight that I did not even have the energy to walk. One morning, I could not get out of bed because my legs were numb. Señorita Alicia sent me to the hospital in Facatativá. I remembered that Señorita Marielita had died there.

When the doctor saw me, he knew at once that I was quite ill. My eyes were turning yellow, and he told me that I was developing hepatitis. I stayed in the hospital for four days, and Señorita Anita came to visit me while I was there. She brought me lots of clothes and other presents to show me how sorry she was. "Maria Luisa," she said quietly, "I am a bad person for saying you were pregnant. I did not know that you had problems with your liver. Can you forgive me?"

I nodded weakly. "Yes, Señorita," I said. "I forgive you."

"Thank you, Maria. You are a good girl. When you leave the hospital, I want you to stay at the boys' grange here in Facatativá until you are fully recovered."

In that grange, there were about fifty children, three teachers, one director, three older girls, and a cook. The director was a lady named Elvira, and she liked to talk to me. She seemed to genuinely love me and would say to everyone that I looked like her little sister. That grange was very famous for its pear trees.

Above: A picture of the boys and I
at the grange of Facatativa

Father Luna came to visit while I was there, and after speaking with Elvira for a few minutes, he asked for me.

I knew he would do that; I knew his routine. When we were alone, he hugged me and said, "I am very sorry for what has happened to you. I hope that you recover soon." But although his words indicated that he was concerned about me, he really didn't care that I was so sick. He started to kiss me and to whisper sweet comments. I was too weak to stop him—I just shook in his arms, letting him touch me and kiss me. When he was done, he asked me to leave the room.

During those days I became very depressed. I wanted to go away, somewhere no one knew anything about me, especially

Father Luna. His behavior was making me more and more frightened—and angry. I thought that I was committing a mortal sin because I allowed him to touch me. The nuns had taught us that anything related to sex was a mortal sin, that even thoughts about sex were a sin. I was very concerned, but I had no one to talk to about my worries.

I recovered quickly, thanks to God, and Señorita Anita came to bring me back to the grange of San Francisco. When she arrived, however, Señorita Elvira asked her to leave me where I was. "The weather in San Francisco is too hot," she argued. "Maria will become sick again. Besides, the girl who mends the clothes here is leaving us. We need Maria Luisa here."

Señorita Anita thought for a moment. "I will call you with my answer," she said. Señorita Elvira did not have to wait long for the call. Señorita Anita's decision was that I would stay there in Facatativá, and she would send my belongings very soon.

Once again, my life had been decided for me. I thought about Lulu the parrot and about Tito. I knew I could write him a letter to let him know where I was, but it would be hard not to have Lulu with me. I loved that parrot.

Señorita Elvira was very good to me. She showed me around the town and took me to mass each day in its beautiful church. And because I now was living in the town where Señorita Marielita was buried, I was able to pray at her grave and decorate it with flowers.

A few days after Señorita Anita left, a truck driver came with all my belongings, and with a message from Señorita Alicia. "She says that if you ever want to return, she will be waiting for you." I was glad to hear that Señorita Alicia thought so fondly of me, but then the driver said he also had bad news for me. Lulu had her wings clipped so that she couldn't fly away, so I was told that my dear Lulu had climbed up into an avocado tree, and had gone up too high and fell. Lulu's fall was really bad and she ended up dying the following day. I was very sad to hear this; Lulu had been my best friend.

Señorita Anita called Señorita Elvira one day to ask if we would visit a woman who was in the hospital in Facatativá. When we went to visit her, I recognized her right away as the mother of one of the girls from my little grange in Alban. Her name was Lucrecia. She had high blood pressure that the doctors were trying to control.

We visited Lucrecia often and brought her fruits, which made her very happy. One afternoon the cook named Carmen, and I went to visit her. Lucrecia asked Carmen if she would make her some pigeon soup. Carmen promised to do so—we had many pigeons in the grange—and she brought it the following day.

"Could I try some?" I asked. "I've never tasted that kind of soup."

"No," Carmen replied rather rudely. "You can't have any. This soup was made especially for the sick lady."

When Lucrecia saw us bringing the soup, she got very happy. But when she started to eat it, she quickly pushed it away. "It's too salty," she explained. "I can't have salt because of my blood pressure."

Carmen scoffed. "Oh, a little bowl of soup won't hurt you. Have some more."

Lucrecia really wanted that soup; I could tell that she was trying to decide what to do. Finally, she said, "All right. Just don't say anything to the nurses." With that, she ate the whole bowl of soup. She thanked us, and then we went back to the grange.

I went to the kitchen to see if there was any soup left—I really wanted to try it. There was a little left in the pot, so I took a spoonful. As soon as it was in my mouth, I was disgusted by how salty it was. "Why did you use so much salt?" I asked.

But she didn't answer me. She just poured the rest of the soup in the sink.

The following day a nurse called to let us know that Señora Lucrecia had passed away during the night. I wondered if the salty soup had had anything to do with her death, but no one would ever know—we never told the nurse that Lucrecia had eaten it.

12

One afternoon not long after Lucrecia's death, Señorita Anita came to talk with Señorita Elvira.

"I've come to ask if you want to be the director of a new grange," she said. "It's located near Bogotá, and it's called Engativa."

"Yes, I would like that," Señorita Elvira said. "May I bring Maria Luisa with me?"

Señorita Anita agreed and said that we were to leave in a month.

A few days later, I saw a girl who had been with me at my little grange, Blanca. We hugged each other because we were so happy to see each other again. "I'm twenty-one years old now," Blanca said. "I live with my aunt in the village, and I work at the post office. What a surprise to see you here!"

She added that Father Luna visited her often and that he was her aunt's good friend. That did not surprise me; I knew that Father Luna liked to spend time with young girls. We said good-bye and made plans to see each other the following Sunday.

Carmen had a baby girl named Clarita. A week before Señorita Elvira and I were to leave for Engativa, Carmen came running in to tell us that she had found her baby girl dead. We all rushed to her room, unable to believe it was true, but there was the baby's lifeless body in the bed.

"How did this happen"? Señorita Elvira cried.

"I don't know," Carmen insisted. "I just found her that way."

Señorita Elvira narrowed her eyes. "That sounds very strange to me. The child was sleeping with you in the same bed. How could you not know what happened?"

Carmen insisted that the baby was dead when she first looked at her that morning. But she did not shed a tear while she was telling us this.

Señorita Anita placed Elvira in charge of the funeral. She sent one of the big girls out to buy the coffin, and another girl and I were in charge of bathing and dressing the dead girl's body. We made her look really beautiful.

When we tried to put her in the coffin, however, we realized that it was too small for her—her legs would not fit in the box.

"I'll go get another coffin," the girl working with me offered.

"That's not necessary," Carmen answered. Then she folded the girl's legs, almost breaking them as she adjusted the little body so that it would fit inside the coffin.

The funeral was very sad for me. During that year I had lost Lulu and Señora Lucrecia, and now this little girl. There were too many sad things happening.

The following day I asked if anyone wanted to pick pears with me. Carmen accepted the offer, and we went down the hill to gather the fruit. We found lots of pears on the ground, and picked some more, and then we sat near the tree to eat them. Carmen seemed quite happy, which seemed odd to me—since she'd buried her baby the day before.

"Do you miss the baby?" I asked.

She didn't respond; she just kept eating pears.

"It was such a pity that she had to die. It was such a sad—"

"She had to die!" Carmen insisted suddenly. "She was my father's daughter—she had to die!"

I was speechless, utterly confused. If the baby had been Carmen's father's, who was the mother? I was naïve. It didn't occur to me that Carmen's father had forced himself on her and made her pregnant. It did occur to me, however, that Carmen had likely taken the baby's life. I remembered the soup she'd made for Señora Lucrecia, and I was suddenly afraid of her, knowing now that she was capable of harming somebody. I thanked God that I was leaving in a couple of days.

When Señorita Elvira arrived at the new grange in Engativa, we were excited to see the big house and its surroundings. I was astonished by the beauty of the place. In addition to the huge and lovely house, there were cows, horses, pigs, hens, and many rabbits. I was to share my room with two other girls. Señorita Elvira was delighted with her room. In one area were Father Luna's and Señorita Anita's rooms, plus two other extra rooms. On the other side there were the teachers' rooms, the classrooms, and the lunch room. In the back were the boys' dorms and other classrooms. Señorita Anita introduced us to the teachers and their pupils. The teachers were very polite, and there were not that many children—maybe forty. The director's name was Jeronimo, and he was an older man.

My job there was to mend and sew the children's clothes. That was all I was assigned to do; there were two cooks, and other girls were in charge of washing clothes and cleaning.

It was during those days at the Engativa grange that I heard the news: John F. Kennedy, the president of the United States, had been killed. Everybody was very sad. Classes were canceled that day because everybody wanted to listen to the radio and follow the news. We had all loved the president because of the many good things he had done for our country, especially in Bogotá. He had helped to build many houses for low-income families, and he had sent food to the schools. We listened to the report of his funeral on the radio, and we paid attention to every single detail—the voice of the news reporter, the galloping of the horses.

Some of the teachers at the grange would share their magazines, and I loved to read them, even if they were old magazines. I loved to learn about the lives of famous people like Marilyn Monroe, Sophia Loren, the Beatles, and Elizabeth Taylor. One day the director and a couple of girls, including myself, heard music coming from across a field near the grange. Curious, we climbed the fence and began to cross. We were never afraid of the cows that grazed there. Every time we'd been near them before that day, they'd ignored us, looking down and eating grass. For that reason, we were terrified to turn around and see all of them, maybe about fifteen cows, running toward us. They were only about fifty feet away from us and were running very fast. There was no place to hide, and the gate was too far to be reached. We started running, but the director asked us to stop. Frantically taking his shirt off, he turned around to face them. Waving his shirt at the cows, he was able to calm them down and to change their direction. Thanks to the director, we were safe. Every time we remembered that situation, it was hard for us to believe that we had almost been trampled by a herd of cows. The music was coming from a festival that was taking place across the field.

About four months went by without any letters from Tito, which was very strange. I had given him my new address in many different letters.

By this time, I was about eighteen years old. Father Luna continued to give me his private "advice," or at least that was what Señorita Elvira thought. The only time I got a reprieve from his attentions was once when a girl name Julia came to stay for a couple of days. She was waiting for Señorita Anita to bring her to another grange. Father Luna was visiting and asked for a private meeting with her. I was excused from my own private meeting with him that day, and I felt as if a heavy rock had been lifted from my shoulders. I felt bad for Julia, of course, but I still felt happy for myself.

One day the man in charge of bringing the groceries brought me a couple of letters from Tito; Señorita Alicia had sent them to me. I noticed that all of them had been opened, and I did not like that. Señorita Alicia did not have the right to read my letters—I was not under her custody anymore. Still, I supposed, she thought she was protecting me.

Tito wrote that he was very concerned about not receiving a reply from me. I quickly sent him a letter letting him know where I was living. I also told him about my liver illness and many other things I had gone through, except what was going on with Father Luna.

About four months went by, and I did not receive any letters from Tito. I thought that was suspicious—I had written him with my new address several times. One day I was mending the children's clothes when some of the kids came to tell me that there was a man looking for me. When I went to see who was asking for me, I was surprised to see that it was Tito! I was delighted to see him, but he seemed quite upset.

"Why haven't you responded to my letters?" he asked. "Why didn't you tell me about moving out of the San Francisco grange? Are you trying to avoid me? I went to look for you in San Francisco, and somebody told me that you were here."

"Oh, Tito!" I cried, anxious that he'd thought I'd been ignoring him. I explained to him about my illness and how sick I had been. "But I sent letters with the drivers—and paid them to deliver them! You didn't get them?"

We both understood then that neither of us had received the letters we'd been writing. His facial expression changed as I explained everything. Then he took my hand and held it in his. "I've missed you so much!" he said.

At that moment, as we stood together, Señorita Elvira walked in and saw us together. Her face looked very stern. "Who is this man, Maria Luisa?"

I quickly snatched my hands away from Tito. "This is my friend Tito, Señorita. I have not seen him in a long while because he has been in the army."

Señorita Elvira nodded. "I have heard Maria Luisa talk about you. I know that she has written many letters to you." She stared at him for a moment, as if she were appraising him, and then said, "The next time you want to see Maria Luisa, you need to ask my permission first."

"Yes, Señorita," Tito agreed.

"You may go visit in the dining room," she pronounced, and I thought I saw her lips start to curl into a smile before she turned away.

Tito had brought many chocolates, which I loved, but the even bigger surprise was a box he pulled out of his pocket, containing a ring with a cluster of red rubies. He put it on my finger. It was a little big for me, but I didn't care—no one had ever given me jewelry. I knew that he truly loved me, and I loved him. We were so involved in our conversation that we did not notice the many eyes watching us. When we finally looked around the room, we saw many faces in the windows. We started laughing at the sight, and we knew that the room was too big for anyone to have heard our conversation.

"Do you know anything about your relatives?" Tito asked suddenly.

"No," I said sadly. "I don't know anything about them."

"One day," he promised, "I'm going to look for them ..." He put his hand on top of mine, and looking into my eyes, he continued, "... after we get married."

I could not believe that he wanted to marry me! I started to laugh. "Yes, after we get married! Then we will look for my family."

He kept looking into my eyes as he asked, "Are you agreeing with what I said?"

I nodded. "Yes, Tito."

Then he surprised me even more. "I bought a piece of land near San Francisco, and I've already built a house there. That will be our home."

I was amazed by everything that was happening to me. Tito then asked who was in charge of me.

"That would be Señorita Anita. She is like a mother to me. She has taken care of me since I was about seven."

"Then I'm going to talk to her in Bogotá. I'm going to tell her that I want to marry you. I'll be back in a month—with Señorita Anita's permission!" He kissed me on the cheek. "Everything will move faster than you expect—you'll see. I love you so much." We left the dining room and he said good-bye, assuring me that he would be back soon.

There were so many people watching us in the dining room that after Tito left, Señorita Elvira told me he could not visit often because he caused too much distraction.

"We weren't doing anything to cause distraction, Señorita," I responded. "The only difference between my visit with Tito and anyone else's visit is that I never stood by the windows, watching them and listening to their conversations."

Señorita Elvira laughed at that. "Well, Maria," she said, "I see that you are smarter than I'd imagined."

About two weeks later, Father Luna made another of his regular visits. After making sure that Señorita Elvira had everything under control, he asked to see me in his room. I had to obey, but when I stepped inside, I did not close the door.

"Please close the door, Maria," he said gently, "I want to speak with you."

"I think it's better if I leave it open," I bravely responded.

But he stood up very quickly and shoved the door shut. He then gave me a gentle hug. "Someone told me that you have a boyfriend."

"Yes, that's true."

He hugged me more tightly. "Who is this boyfriend? Where does he live?"

I looked away from him. I did not want to give him much information about Tito.

He took my chin in his hand, forcing me to look at him. "When will your next period take place?" he asked.

I was very surprised by such a question. "Why do you ask me that?"

He shook me hard. "*When will it take place?*"

He was scaring me, and my voice quavered as I answered. "Maybe in … five or six days."

When he heard that, he turned very sweet again. He kissed me and asked me to save a used pad or dirty underwear once my period was gone. This surprised me a lot. I thought that Father Luna must be getting crazy. He kept on kissing me, saying, "Do not fail me in this. I have a grange very far away from here, and if you are not a good girl for me, I will have to send you there. Nobody will know anything about you for a long time." He kissed me once more and then released me from his grasp. "I will come back for the things I asked for in seven days." He grabbed my arm as I started to walk away, and for the first time he said, "No one must know about our conversation in this room. You are excused."

This problem with Father Luna was making me so depressed that I wanted to disappear. On that same day, the delivery truck came and left the *Mundo* (a newspaper). I started flipping through the pages and saw an ad—someone was looking for a nanny. The job included room and board, and good pay. I cut the ad out of the paper and put it in my pocket. I was considering running away to escape from Father Luna. But how would I do that? I would have had to walk at least ten minutes to get the bus, and I was afraid that Senorita Elvira would see me walking to the bus stop through her window. I would be in trouble if she found out I'd left the grange without permission. Still, I liked the idea of running away, and I almost could see it happening.

That night I went to bed with many thoughts in my head. If I left the grange, I could lose Tito, because I could not tell him where I was going. I could wait for Tito to come back for me, as he had promised, but I did not want to see Father Luna again. I decided that I was going to ask Dolores, the cook, to go shopping with me, and my plan was to separate from her when we got into town. In the morning, Dolores happily agreed. My plan seemed to be working, until I had to ask Señorita Elvira for her authorization to go shopping.

"No, Maria," she said, "You cannot go shopping during the week. You have a lot of work to do. The best day to go shopping would be on Saturday."

I left very sad, because it was on Saturday that Father Luna was supposed to return. I returned to my workroom and started to cry. Dolores heard me and tried to comfort me. Then Señorita Elvira came in the room. She smiled. "All right, Maria," she said, "If you finish all your work, you can go shopping tomorrow. Don't forget that all the children need to have their clothes ready for the weekend."

I hugged her. "Thank you for changing your mind!"

For me, it was done; the following day, I would go to the place listed in the ad. I asked God to help me face any adversity. I hardly slept that night, thinking about Tito and how I could lose him. Thinking about Señorita Anita made me sad, too; she was like a mother to me. Still, it was the only way I had to get away from Father Luna. I never even thought about telling her about what was going on, knowing they would never believe me over Father Luna, it would have just created a big mess.

Thursday morning was beautiful—sunny and warm. We left for the city, which was about half an hour away from the grange. Once we were on the bus, I told Dolores about my plan.

"How could you do that?" she asked angrily. "Don't count on me to help you, not when you're leaving a place where people take such a good care of you!"

"I'm sorry, Dolores, but I—"

"You don't know how hard life is outside of the grange," she insisted. "You'll be sorry you ever thought of this plan. I'm not going to go with you to that place in the ad. I'm going to shop for my kids. You can go anywhere you want, but it'll be without me!"

I sighed. "Please don't say anything at the grange."

"Do you think I'm stupid? I'm not going to say something and be blamed for your leaving." She turned to look at me, and she seemed calmer now. "Good luck, Maria. I'll just say that we got lost in the city. I looked for you, but when I couldn't find you, I decided to go back to the grange."

We said good-bye then. I never told her where I was going; it was my secret. I took a taxi and went to the place in the ad. I was sure that it was going to be a family's house, but it was an office that placed girls in domestic service. When I got there, there were four girls waiting to be called. I sat in that office waiting for my turn, too, without speaking to anybody. After about five minutes, a well-dressed lady came into the room. She looked at everyone and then asked me if I had a job.

"I don't have one yet," I answered. "I haven't had a chance to talk to anybody at the office yet."

"Come outside with me," she said. Once outside, she asked if I wanted to go with her. "I have three girls who need someone to care for them, and I also need a few things to be done in the house."

"Yes, I like children; I'd love to take care of them."

"I can pay you 180 pesos monthly."

That sounded like a lot of money to me. At the grange, I only earned thirty pesos a month. "Thank you," I said. "I would like to work for you."

"Where are your belongings? I can take you to get them."

Just thinking of going back to the grange gave me goose bumps, and I panicked. "I … I … my belongings are.…"

"Yes? Where are they?"

I took a deep breath. "I have them at a little village called Engativá."

"Ah, I know where that is. Get in my car—we'll go get your things."

I could not believe how easy it was. I didn't know how everyone would react when they saw me getting my stuff, but I was on my way.

"How long have you been at the grange?" she asked. "What do you do there?"

"I've lived at one of Father Luna's granges since I was very little."

"Ah, yes, Father Luna. I met him once at a special event—an event to raise money for poor people."

I wasn't really paying attention as she described the banquet at which she'd met Father Luna. "I'm leaving the grange, but no one knows about it," I confessed.

"I see. Well, don't be afraid. How old are you?"

"I'll soon be nineteen."

We kept talking, and she told me that she was from Spain and that her name was Ana Gomez. She lived in a town called Chico with her husband, three daughters, and two dogs. We were almost to Engativá, and I started to get nervous.

"Calm down," she said. "The only thing they can do is yell at you. They can't do anything else—they aren't your parents. Besides, you're old enough to be on your own."

When we got to the grange, everything was peaceful and quiet, mostly because all the children were in their classrooms. I went to my room, grabbed a bag, and very quickly started to put all of my stuff inside it. Suddenly, one of the girls came in and asked why I was packing my stuff. But I just kept on collecting my belongings.

Then Señorita Elvira came in. "What are you doing, Maria Luisa? What is going on?"

I turned to face her. "I am leaving for good." With that, I walked briskly from the room. She tried to hold me by the arm but I pulled free and ran toward the car.

"Maria! Wait! What will I tell Father Luna and Señorita Anita?"

Once I was safely in the car, I called back to her. "Tell them that I am thankful for everything and that I am going to be fine. Tell them not to worry."

At that moment, Señora Ana drove away as fast as a rocket. As we continued down the road, she was laughing out loud—I had been so worried, and everything had turned out to be so easy.

I, on the other hand, started to think about what I had done—I had left the grange, which had been like my home, and the people, who were like a family to me, since I was seven years old. I had learned so many things in that place. I wished I had been able to thank Señorita Anita for all the things she'd done for me. There, at my little grange, I had lived the best days of my life. I had celebrated my first Christmas there, and I'd played with my first doll. That was the place where I'd learned to pray, and even though there were some hard times, I didn't mind: it was part of life. My eyes were full of tears. I couldn't hold them back, because there were so many memories.

Señora Ana rubbed my shoulder. "Do you regret what you've just done? Do you want me to take you back?"

"No," I answered. Then I told her about the part of my life that I had lived at the grange in Alban: I had arrived at the grange when I was seven, in August 1952. Now it was 1964. I was nineteen, and I was on my own. From now on, I didn't have anyone to look out for me. I had taken one of the most important steps in my whole life, so I had to be responsible for my own actions.

13

Señora Ana's house was beautiful. At the front she had a lush garden with a lovely entrance. The furniture was gorgeous, and she had a big piano. There were spiral stairs that led to the second floor and a crystal chandelier hanging from the ceiling. There were so many rooms, I could barely keep count, and they included special rooms set aside for the maid, the gardener, and other service personnel. There was also a bedroom for me. It was a beautiful room, with its own bathroom and pretty furniture.

"Why don't you unpack your things and relax for a while?" Señora Ana suggested. "After that, I'll show you the rest of the house."

After putting my stuff away—it didn't take long, as I had left many of my things at the grange because I'd left in such a hurry—I found Señora Ana, and she showed me the areas of the house for which I would be responsible. There was a large living area, which was the family room, and there were also four more bedrooms, which were very large. All of the bedrooms had their own bathrooms. I had never seen a house like this in my whole life—it was a mansion.

Coming down from the stairs I saw a water fountain surrounded by many plants. The ceiling had a skylight, which provided them with sun. She then showed me the patio behind the house. It was quite good-sized, with more flowers and greenery, and chairs with umbrellas.

Her daughters came home from their school then, and Señora Ana introduced me to them: Ana, who was about thirteen, had light blonde hair and blue eyes; Cuty, who was about ten, was a little chubby and had very black hair and green eyes; and Merly, who was about eight, was a beautiful child with blonde hair, blue eyes, and an angel's face. They all gave me their schoolbags so I could bring them to their rooms. After that, the girls started asking me all kinds of questions about myself.

They wanted me to play with them outside, but Señora Ana said no, it was time for me to iron clothes.

Soon, Señora Ana's husband, Santiago, arrived. He was very tall and seemed a lot older than her. "How clever of you to have found an employee so soon," he said.

"Yes," she agreed, "and I'm proud to say that I did not even have to pay for her—that is, I didn't have to pay the employment office to find someone for me. Maria didn't report herself to the employment office; she was just sitting there, waiting to be helped, when I saw her!" They laughed a lot about that. She also told him about the dramatic experience of going to the grange to collect my belongings.

At around nine o'clock that night, Señora Ana told me that I could go to sleep. She handed me a list of things that I needed to do the following day, which started at six in the morning.

Once in my room, I closed the door and thanked God for the wonderful things that were happening to me. I was very happy that I'd had the courage to escape from the grange. I was even happier that nobody knew where I was, and the city was too big for anyone to find me.

I was relieved that Father Luna would not be able to molest me again, but sad that I had lost communication with Tito. I could not write to him anymore, and I hoped he would not think too unkindly of me. He had been my first love, and I would never forget him. He had been so kind and respectful.

The following morning, I took a shower and got dressed, and when I opened the door of my room, I came face-to-face with the dogs Señora Ana had told me about. They were big dogs, and I was more than a little afraid of them. I tried to get to the kitchen, but the one named Danty chased after me and tore my dress. I managed to get into the kitchen and close the door, but my dress was completely torn. When Señora Ana came downstairs, she yelled at the dog and took him outside to the patio.

My morning chores consisted of waking up at six in the morning, taking the dogs outside, cleaning up after the dogs in the garage, going to the store to get fresh bread for breakfast, waking the girls, and helping them get dressed. This last detail was not an easy task, because they would try on many clothes before choosing what they wanted to wear. They would just throw the rejected clothes on the floor, and I had to pick them up and put them back in the closet. I had to put on Merly's shoes and do her hair. I also had to get their schoolbags ready. After that, I had to go downstairs to get breakfast ready. Then Señora Ana would take the girls to the school in her car, and her husband would leave at the same time to go to his office.

After breakfast, I had to make the beds, clean the bathrooms, run the vacuum, clean the family room, and clean the stairs. After that I had to water the plants and clean the whole first floor. At lunchtime, everybody would come back to eat. It had to happen really fast, because the girls needed to go back to school and their father to his office. Sometimes, Señora Ana would take me grocery shopping, and I was in charge of pushing the cart. Once we were back in the house, I had to do the laundry and hang it on the clothesline outside. I learned that I needed to give some kind of treat to Danty when I went out to the patio—then he would not bite me.

I spent most of my time ironing—the amount of clothing this family went through was just ridiculous—but I also had to fold the laundry and bring it upstairs to their closets. Once the girls were back from school, I had to stop ironing to help them put their schoolbags and shoes away. Dinner was always a light meal; it consisted of sandwiches. I lost a lot of weight and was hungry sometimes, because the portions were pretty small. For that reason, every time I would get the bread for breakfast, I would buy something for myself, too. Señora Anna told me that I had a free Sunday every two weeks to go anywhere I wanted to go. I had no place to go, so I asked her if I could stay at the house.

"That would be a good idea," she responded. "You could organize the closets and do other little things that you can't do during the week."

The work was a little hard, but I was used to that, and I was receiving a good salary. Sometimes I would talk with the girls from the house next door. They worked with a couple who had two children and three maids. They used to tell me that my boss was a cheap person, and that was why Señora Ana had only one maid to do all the housework. It was a lot of work for only one person, and the salary was too low.

I thought they were paying me a lot, although I agreed that it was a lot of work for just one person. The only thing I did not do was cook, but I did wash the dishes and clean the kitchen after each meal. I did not have time to think about Tito or

Father Luna or the grange, because as soon as my head touched the pillow, I would fall asleep.

One Sunday I left really early to visit a church that was only five blocks from the house. I thanked God for every good thing he had given me, and for the peace I was enjoying. All of my problems were behind me. After mass, I stayed seated in the church. Everything there was so silent, and I could think about my life and my family—and about Tito. Actually, I was feeling rather lonely. I was used to the noise at the grange and to being surrounded by many children and people. My life had changed, and it was taking me a while to get used to it.

After about eight months, I started to take more advantage of my days off—I learned to travel on the public bus. One day I decided to see if my old school, where I'd gone with Rosa and the other two girls from the grange, was still running. We'd found it so exciting to be going to Bogotá. I remembered spending Sundays listening to music and mingling with other girls. So I took a bus there one Sunday, and when I got there I found a girl who remembered me. Her name was Tina, and when we saw each other, we hugged each other and started jumping with happiness. I was even happier when I saw Mother Cecilia. She told me that she was happy to see me again, and that she was in charge of the salon and the girls who came to visit from the outside. I was delighted to be in that place and to see my friends again. One more time I thanked God for guiding me back there. That day I listened to some music and danced with my friends. I had a marvelous afternoon. We all exchanged phone numbers and promised to see each other every two weeks.

When I got back to Señora Ana's house, she was concerned because it was late and she didn't know where I was. The girls were also concerned, because they were waiting for me to do their nails.

"I'm sorry you were worried," I said. "I got busy—I bumped into some old friends and lost track of time." Señora Ana seemed happy for me.

The housework became easier with time. I was gaining experience, and the whole family really loved me—even the dogs.

Every Thursday afternoon, the piano teacher would come to teach the girls. She was a very elegant lady. That was my favorite day, because I enjoyed listening to the piano, especially the songs from Spain. They were beautiful. The girls also received dancing lessons. Sometimes they would go to the school for the dancing lessons, and sometimes the teacher would come to their house. These girls knew how to dance very well already, and they were very skilled with the castanets. I admired that a lot. I tried to do all my work quickly so that I could spend more time watching them.

I returned to my old school on the following Sunday, and I was excited to see my old friends again, especially Tina. That day, there were a lot of girls at the salon. We all talked and listened to music. Mother Cecilia was there, and she asked me if I was happy where I was working and how much I was receiving as a salary. She also wanted to know about the type of work that I was doing.

After I told her about my job, she said, "If you want, I can find you a better job with a better salary and with fewer responsibilities."

"Thank you, Mother," I said. "I'll think about it."

I wanted to visit Rosa, the girl who had become a nun. I went upstairs, and once I got to the cloister—the room only the nuns could enter—I rang the bell. A nun came to greet me, and

I asked for Rosa. After about thirty minutes, Rosa came out, but she did not seem to recognize me. How disappointing! I had wanted to ask her many questions about life in the convent and share our memories of growing up, but she acted as if I were a stranger. I said good-bye, and I almost cried because of her indifference. It was sad to think my special old friend had become a cold and frustrated woman.

I returned to the salon and enjoyed my time with the girls, especially Tina. Later, when I went to say good-bye to Mother Cecilia, she reminded me to think about our conversation. I promised that I would.

When I got back to Señora Ana's, the girls were waiting for me. I did not want to think about leaving them. I felt protected in that place. Señora Ana had changed my life completely; I felt that I had nothing to worry about. I had finally obtained physical and mental peace.

I continued to get together with the girls at my old school every other Sunday. One day Mother Cecilia told me that she had something very important to share with me. She took me aside, where the others could not hear our conversation. "I have found good work for you, Maria. It is at the Italian Embassy. They need a girl to be a waitress, and the pay is very good. It's a very nice place. You don't have to worry if you don't know anything about being a waitress. They'll train you. I would suggest that you not let this opportunity pass without really thinking about it. If you want to take the job, you'll need to start next week."

I stayed quiet for a while—I didn't know how to respond.

Then Mother Cecilia said, "You have the whole day to think about it, but you need to tell me before you leave here today."

I asked Tina for her advice, because I was confused.

"Well, it's a privilege to work at the embassy, so that might be the best thing. It's good pay, and it sounds like you don't have to do much."

I thought about it for a couple of hours and finally decided that I was going to take the job Mother Cecilia had recommended. She was very excited and told me that I would not regret it, that it was going to be a great place for me.

"I just don't know how I'm going to tell Señora Ana," I admitted.

"I think you should just tell her that you found another job, and that you're giving her a week's notice. If you have any problems, you can call me at the convent right away."

When I returned to Señora Ana's house, she and the girls were waiting for me, as they always did. I greeted them politely, but I knew I had to tell her my news. I didn't say anything that night, but the next day, after finishing my chores, I felt strong enough to approach her. I told her that I had to leave because the nuns had found me another job.

She got very upset and didn't let me finish talking. "The girls and I love you, Maria!" she shouted. "How can you do this to us?" She stormed around the house for a few minutes and then asked me if it was my final decision.

I nodded my head slowly. "Yes, it is."

"Then gather your things right away and get out! I want you to leave this instant, and I don't want to see you ever again!"

I was very scared as I gathered my things. "May I use the phone?" I asked meekly—I needed to call Mother Cecilia.

"*No!* Get out of here *immediately!*" And without another word, she shoved me out the door and slammed it behind me. I couldn't even say good-bye to the girls. Señora Ana *had* called a taxi for me, however. When it arrived, I asked the driver to take me to the nuns.

When Mother Cecilia saw me, she was surprised but happy. I told her what had happened with Señora Ana, and Mother Cecilia sent me to one of the bedrooms so I could stay there until she was able to take me to the embassy.

"I'm very thankful for everything you've done for me."

She smiled. "It's time for you to relax and have something to eat. Don't worry; everything is going to be fine."

PART III

Life at the Italian Embassy

14

Two days later, the consul's wife, Mrs. Botticelli—came to take me to the embassy. Once there, she explained the job to me—I was to work for the ambassadors, who would come in one month. Meanwhile, I had to learn my duties by heart so that I would know exactly what to do when they arrived.

Above: A picture of me in the front garden
of the Italian Embassy.

Then she introduced me to the other girls who worked there and asked one of them to show me around my new home. The embassy was located north of the city. It was a two-story brick building, surrounded by pine trees and rose gardens.

An iron gate was at the entrance of the embassy and pine trees enclosed the entire property; it looked very elegant. The inside was gorgeous, too, with French furniture, marble staircases, and plush red carpets. The rooms were huge, including the kitchen, which had preparation areas and a butler's bedroom. There were about eight other bedrooms, all of them elegant and well appointed. I was amazed, too, by the number of bathrooms, and I thought absently that I had come a long way from squatting in a field outside the garage where I'd lived with Tia Trinita.

After my tour of the embassy, the girl took me to my room, which I was to share with another girl. I settled in, and quickly became used to the routine. Once a week, a lady would come to show us how to get the table ready for the embassy dinners and how to serve the food in a proper manner. She also told us that we should address the ambassador as Mr. Ambassador or Your Excellency, and his wife as Mrs. Countess—she belonged to the royal family. We were to greet them politely but never walk in front of them or interrupt them when they were talking.

Mrs. Botticelli usually wasn't at the embassy for most of the day, so there wasn't anyone to give us orders. We had a lot of freedom, and we had a lot of free time, too. I sometimes wrote a letter to my aunt Trinita. I still missed her and wished that I could see her again. I didn't know if she'd ever receive my letters—I had no idea where she might be—but I sent them to Santa Teresa and hoped that they might find their way to her somehow.

Mrs. Botticelli told us that the ambassadors would arrive by boat in a few days, so we had to keep the embassy neat and clean. We placed flower arrangements in all the rooms, including the ambassador's bedroom.

My main role was to wait at the table, clean up the dining room, and answer the door and the phone. Magdalena, one of the other girls, was in charge of cleaning the bedrooms and ironing clothes. Elvira, the third girl, was in charge of cooking and doing the laundry.

Finally, the ambassador arrived. Mrs. Botticelli told us to wait in a straight line by the door. We had to greet the ambassador and his wife as soon as they came through the door. The countess entered first; we greeted her, and she responded very politely. Then Mr. Ambassador came in; we greeted him, too, but he walked past us without speaking. He was accompanied by his personal butler, Karupian, who was from India. Perhaps he thought his butler would speak for him, but I thought the ambassador was quite arrogant.

I set the table for dinner, using brand-new dinnerware, and I set everything just the way I had been taught to do. But this dinnerware came with a plate that was shaped differently from those I'd been using to practice. It was in the shape of a "C." I didn't know what it was for, so I placed it right next to the large plate. Then I decided to place a banana right on top of it, since it had that exact shape.

When we started serving dinner; the countess called me over to her. "Maria Luisa, do you see this plate?" she asked, pointing to the C-shaped one. "This plate is for salad, not for bananas."

At that moment the ambassador laughed out loud and his guests did, too. Mrs. Botticelli explained to the countess that it was new dinnerware, and I wasn't familiar with it. But they kept on laughing, even after I apologized; she told me not to worry about it.

The countess had some new uniforms made for me out of fine black silk. The apron was white, with ruffles on the border. It seemed very extravagant to me, but she said the uniform looked very nice on me. She also said that I had beautiful hair and that as long as I kept it well brushed, I didn't have to tie it back in a ponytail.

Within days, the visitors started coming, often with flowers and other gifts. When the countess received a flower arrangement, I was in charge of setting it out for her and placing the card that came along with it on a silver platter. When visitors arrived, they were greeted very courteously by the butler. He sent them to one of the living rooms, and soon afterward the countess came to attend to her visitors. Most of the visitors were other ambassadors or high-society individuals. Sometimes we girls took turns serving with the butler when the guests asked for something to eat or drink. The countess had visitors at least three times a week.

I liked the countess very much, and I think she also liked me; she was always calling me to brush her hair or to help her with her makeup or shoes. I also brought her tea or fruit without her asking, and she was really happy with me. On Sundays I continued to visit the nuns at the school. I told Mother Cecilia that I was very happy. "The countess is a very good person," I told her, "and I am very thankful that you found this job for me."

I also visited my friends, and we listened to a lot of music. We danced and exchanged ideas. I told Tina, my best friend, all about my job at the embassy and how happy I was. The best of all was that they paid me almost double what I had earned with Señora Ana—and it was far less work.

The ambassador began to host grand dinners, and these social events were covered in all the newspapers. I had to set the table; it took me almost three hours, even with the help of the butler. The countess taught me to make lotus flowers with the napkins and to put them in the center of the main plate. The table looked very beautiful, with floral arrangements as the centerpiece. The food was catered, and the caterers, who were dressed in white, always looked very professional.

Around seven in the evening, the guests would begin to arrive for dinner, and my job was to take their coats after the butler welcomed them in. After enjoying drinks and conversation, the guests went to the dining room and sat at their assigned places. The ambassador and the countess would sit at either end of the table, and the special guests sat next to them—when married couples came to dinner, the wife sat at the right hand of the ambassador at one end of the table, and the husband at the right hand of the countess at the other. Many times, the guests would stay late into the night—well past midnight—but even on these nights we couldn't go to sleep until we had finished washing the dishes and silverware and put them away. Sometimes we still hadn't finished at four in the morning. The following day, the countess often gave us extra money and thanked us for having worked so hard all night.

I continued sending letters to my aunt Trinita, but I had no answer in return. Sometimes I thought that maybe she had never returned to our little town of Santa Teresa, and that was why she hadn't answered my letters. I also thought about how big baby José and my brothers must be by now. And I wondered if they ever thought of me, because I thought often of them. How I wished that I could tell them that I was very well and healthy, that I still missed them and hadn't lost hope of seeing them again.

I had already saved a little bit of money from my salary to buy myself a sewing machine. On my days off, I bought material and made myself skirts and dresses. The countess also started to give me clothing to repair. One day, I saw that some of the ambassador's shirts had worn-out collars. I took them off and then replaced them, reversed; now they were in perfect condition. When he realized what I had done, the ambassador sent for me to thank me in person for having fixed his shirts.

One morning, the butler told us that we should go out to the street if we wanted to see the president of France go by. We ran out just in time to see a caravan of motorcycles, followed by the French president's car. The car was a convertible, so we were able to see Charles de Gaulle sitting in it. He was bald and had a very long nose, and he waved to us as he rode past. He was smiling and seemed very friendly and distinguished. I couldn't believe that I had just seen the president from a country as important as France. That night, the ambassador and countess attended a dinner in honor of the French president. As always, the countess sent for me to help her get dressed. She chose a blue princess-style dress that was covered with brilliant jewels. It was so beautiful, it nearly took my breath away, and I asked if I could call Magdalena and Elvira so that they could see her dress. We all stood in awe—the countess looked so beautiful.

Even though I was busy with my work, I didn't stop thinking about my relatives. I decided to send another letter, but this time I sent it to San Luis de Gaseno via Santa Teresa. I thought that if I sent it to a different town, someone might bring this letter to my aunt Trinita.

One day, the countess said that she wanted some special curtains for the family room. She asked me to go to the fabric store to buy some rose satin, because she wanted the curtains to look beautiful and welcoming. She suggested that she and I could make the curtains together, because she didn't know how to sew, but she liked to play with the fabrics. When I returned from my shopping trip, she was happy because I'd chosen the exact color that she had wanted. She had ordered that a large table be placed in the middle of the room, and we used it to measure and cut the fabric. I sat down to sew, and as I worked, she continued to say one word: *Bravo!*

That afternoon, when the ambassador arrived, he asked his wife what she was doing.

"We're making some very elegant curtains for this room," she replied.

The ambassador laughed. "Tomorrow in the newspapers," he teased, "there will be an announcement that says 'Italian Ambassador Opens Curtain Factory!'"

Our work on the curtains took us about two weeks, but when it was all finished, I couldn't believe how beautifully they had turned out. The countess was very pleased, and she marveled at my work.

While sewing curtains, we often chatted. One day she told me that when she was very young, she had lived in England—that was where she had met her husband. They had two children, both now grown. One of them worked for the Italian government, and the other was a sailor. He would be coming into port at Cartagena in a few months. She was planning to have a big party in his honor.

She and the ambassador had recently been in Ceylon, an island very close to India, where he'd also been the Italian ambassador. "It was very beautiful there," she said, "full of flowering trees and a lot of gardens. But it was very hot, and we had to dress in white by day because of the heat."

The couple had also been in Africa as ambassadors: "Would you like to hear a story about that?" she asked.

"Oh yes!" I said. "I love to hear about your travels."

"Well, while we were in Africa," she began, "we went on safari into the jungle. Our guides set up camp for us the first night in a spot in the jungle that was more or less safe. We had other couples along with us on the safari, and one couple brought their children, who were nine and twelve. The children started to play and run everywhere, but the adults were chatting and eating and didn't notice—until suddenly their mother realized that the children had disappeared. Everyone searched for them, but even though they searched all night, we only found one child. The nine-year-old girl was never found. Eventually, we had to assume that a tiger or lion had eaten her."

The countess was almost in tears as she told me this story and how the girl's parents had suffered from their loss. "I've never really recovered from the tragedy either," she admitted. "It's always on my mind, even after all these years."

"I can understand how easily the child got lost," I offered. "When you're in the jungle, it's really easy to get disoriented. All the trees look the same, and if you just turn around once, you're already lost."

She looked at me, surprised. "Why, yes, that's true. How did you know that?"

"When I was very little," I said quietly, "I was in the mountains with my father and my brothers. We were running from the guerrilla warriors."

She seemed quite touched by my story, even though I had only told her a tiny bit of it—I thought it would be a very long story to tell. But I watched her as I shared some of the details, and I thought to myself that she also had some sad stories and some happy ones, just like me.

Once the curtains were up, we put everything back in its place in the salon, and it looked beautiful. The countess spent a lot of time in that room, painting, reading, or talking on the telephone. It was her favorite place—almost magical and enchanting—and I was very happy that I'd had such a large role in making her room so beautiful.

One morning, the mailman arrived and gave me a collection of envelopes, as usual. But on this day, I noticed one that had my name on it—and it had come from Santa Teresa. It was from my aunt Trinita! I couldn't believe my eyes. I already had tears running down my cheeks as I started to read it:

Dear Maria Luisa,

I was very happy to hear from you. Someone from San Luis de Gaseno brought the letter to Santa Teresa, and I was so very happy to receive it. A few months after I took you to Father Luna's grange, Aunt Conchita, the children, and I returned to Santa Teresa. We were not able to survive any longer in Garagoa.

When we got back, the cattle, pigs, and chickens were all gone. Basically, we had lost everything. But it wasn't as dangerous in Santa Teresa anymore. The army was already there and in the surrounding towns. No more guerrillas were around, even though they had killed a lot of people, and a lot more had disappeared. This hadn't happened only in Santa Teresa; it also happened in a lot of other little towns as well. Your father came for you and Eliecer, but when he didn't find you, he got mad at me for taking you to Father

Luna's grange. He took Eliecer and Avelino with him and left. Conchita and I have not heard anything from him in nearly twelve years.

I am married, and now I have a very beautiful girl, who is nine years old. Her name is Gloria.

Please come back to Santa Teresa. I need someone to help me. Aunt Conchita has arthritis and can't take care of the cows or do other jobs. Now, I have only my husband's and José del Carmen's help—he has just turned fifteen.

Lastly, your uncle Oliverio is there in Bogotá. He got married and now has four children. I will include his address for you at the end of this letter. I miss you very much.

Love,

Tia Trinita

I couldn't believe it—after fourteen years, I was reading a letter from my aunt Trinita. It was like a dream to me; I was so happy to have finally received a letter from my aunt but at the same time I was also upset that she did not try to find me. After reading the letter it felt very awkward to me that after so many years she asks me to leave the new life that I had gotten used to. She wanted me to just up and leave everything to go back to the countryside to raise cattle and to help take care of her children. But, what made me really happy was knowing that my uncle Oliverio was here in Bogotá. This filled me with joy, and I thought about going to visit him.

My eyes were still full of tears when I heard the butler call me. The countess wanted to speak with me.

"Maria Luisa," she said as I entered her room, "the ambassador and I are going to the theater to hear a concert by a tenor from Italy. We will be the honored guests. Would you like to come with us to the concert?"

My mouth dropped open and I was practically speechless. Then I composed myself, "I'd love to go! I've never been to a theater in my life! I've never heard a tenor sing in person."

Above: This is the dress that was given to me
by the countess.

The countess smiled at me. "Then we must find you a dress." She took me to her closet. After I tried on a few of her things, she decided that I should wear a black Italian silk dress. It fit me perfectly; the dress hugged my every curve, and it had sleeves that came down to my elbows. The countess was very tall, so I had to take a few inches off. I cut it so that it came a little below my knees. The dress was beautiful. That night, I did my hair in the bouffant style that was popular then, and I wore shoes with very high heels. Magdalena helped me to get dressed and let me borrow some jewelry. Elvira just watched, laughing and calling me Cinderella. I think they were a little jealous that I was invited and not them.

When it was time to leave, the ambassador took one look at me and whistled, and the countess began to applaud. She told me to twirl around, and I did so very slowly, with my arms held up high, playing along with the game. Even the chauffer asked who I was. I was laughing and having a lot of fun. At the theater, I had a special place to sit, where the countess could see me from the honored-guest balcony. I felt like a princess.

The tenor was incredible; his voice was marvelous, and so strong. It was an amazing performance. On the way back to the embassy, I thanked the countess and ambassador for inviting me. "This was one of the most wonderful experiences of my life," I said.

"Italy is famous for its tenors and artists," she responded. "I'm glad you enjoyed it."

That night I could barely sleep; so many great things had happened that day. I thought a lot about what my aunt Trinita had told me in her letter, about my going back to Santa Teresa to live and work with them in the fields. I loved her, but I had no intention of returning to live there for any reason; it brought back bad memories. Maybe I would go back to visit, but never to live.

15

I waited very anxiously for Sunday to come—I was going to visit my uncle Oliverio. I remembered how much I had admired him in his uniforms when I was little and how well he had always treated me. He'd always told me how pretty I was and how nice my long and curly hair was. He always had kind things to say to me. When Sunday came, I called a taxi to take me to Oliverio's house. On the way, I started chatting with the driver. I said that I would like to stop at a store to buy some candies for the children. When we started driving again, the driver asked, "Do you work at the embassy?"

"Yes, I do," I answered.

"Do you … have a boyfriend?"

I giggled. "No, I don't."

"Then could I have your phone number?"

I gave it to him very happily, because I felt full of optimism at that moment.

When we arrived at the address, I found a very little house attached to another house. From the doorway, which was very low, I could see some children playing in the patio—these were my cousins. There was no bell, so I waited for them to see me. The biggest girl came to open the door for me.

"Does a Señor Oliverio live here?" I asked.

"Yes," said the biggest girl. "That's our father."

Then a very beautiful woman came out of a room and gave me a stern look. "Who are you?" she demanded.

"I am Maria Luisa Morales," I answered.

She blinked a couple times and then said, "How do you know Oliverio?"

"I'm his niece."

"He's working," she said, "and he won't be home for three hours. How did you find us?"

"I got a letter from Tia Trinita," I answered. "She gave me the address."

Then she told me to show her the letter from Aunt Trinita; it seemed like she didn't believe what I was saying.

"Well, I don't have it with me, but I'm part of your family."

The children stared at me, and then the oldest girl spoke. "Where do you live? Why haven't we ever seen you before?"

I explained a little to them, and I gave them the treats. They thanked me and were very happy.

Finally, their mother said, "My name is Natividad. Oliverio has never mentioned you."

"Maybe he doesn't remember me," I suggested, "but I remember him."

Natividad watched me with malice as I played with the children. I asked them their names, and the oldest one said that her name was Hermelinda and that she was nine years old. Tears came to my eyes, because I hadn't heard this name in such a long time. Next in line was Mauricio; he was six years old. Then it was Patricia, who was four, and Nestor, who was six months old. Later, another boy, Venancio, who was about thirteen years old, came home. He was Natividad's son from a previous marriage.

The three hours passed by very quickly. I was having a great time with the children, when my uncle Oliverio finally came in, dressed in his uniform. He started hugging the children, then greeted me politely and went over to Natividad, who looked quite surprised.

"Don't you recognize her?" she asked.

He looked at me more intensely. "No. Should I?"

I smiled at him. He looked much the same to me, but I had changed a great deal. "I am Maria Luisa, the daughter of your brother Sergio."

When he heard my words, he ran toward me and hugged me, telling me how stupid he was not to have recognized me. He kept looking at me again and again. "I cannot believe what I see!" he said excitedly.

Then he started asking me thousands of questions. There didn't seem to be enough time to speak. I told him that after many years of trying to locate my aunt Trinita, I had finally found her, and she had sent me his address.

"Natividad," he said, voice breaking with emotion, "it has been so many years since I heard anything about my brother or his family. It is a miracle that she is here now. I had assumed that they were lost forever." Then he properly introduced me to his children and to his wife.

We continued talking about Aunt Trinita and the rest of the family. He took my hands and told me that he wanted to show me something that would make me very happy. We went to his room, where he pointed to a photograph on the wall. It was my grandmother Hermelinda. When I saw the photo, I exploded into sobs and fell to my knees. Never in my life had I felt so much emotion—all the horrible memories I had of her came flooding back: how she scolded me and hit me without compassion, how she hated me, how she took away my food, and how she gave me away.

Uncle Oliverio and the children just watched me, surprised. Then he patted my shoulder and said, "Don't cry for your grandmother. She was very good, and now she's in heaven, blessing us. I understand that you miss her a lot."

In truth, of course, I didn't miss her at all. But I wasn't going to tell him that.

It was already getting very late, and I had to return to the embassy. I said good-bye and promised the children that I would return very soon. On the way back, in the taxi, I had a lot of time to think about my life as a child and all that had happened to me. But I also thought a lot about everything that happened to me that day. I was so happy that now I had family nearby. Now, I no longer felt so alone.

I arrived back at the embassy around ten o'clock at night, and because it was so late, the countess had been very worried about me. But I told her that I had been visiting my uncle, because I'd recently discovered that he was living in Bogotá. She seemed relieved, but she asked me not to be out so late at night. "It's not safe for a young woman your age to be outside on the streets after a certain time," she said gently. The butler and the other girls also reproached me for being late. I had not realized that everyone was so concerned about me. I smiled at all of them and thanked them for taking such care of me.

My friend Tina called, saying she wanted to tell me something really important. We planned to meet on Sunday, at the college. The taxi driver who had taken me to Uncle Oliverio's also called—to ask me out. He wanted us to go see a movie and take a walk in the park. All of a sudden, I had a very busy social life! It seemed that everything came all at once. Just a couple of years ago, I'd had no one to talk to. Now, I not only had a family member living close to me, but I had many friends and even a guy who was interested in me. I was living the best days of my life. Every once in a while I thought of Tito; I still missed him.

On Sunday I went to see Tina. She told me that the family for whom she was working wanted to move to the United States—and they wanted to bring her along. They wanted her to take care of their children in Boston, and they wanted to move in two weeks. I could hardly believe my ears! She was moving to a faraway place, to another country! Her mother and family lived there in Bogotá.

"Are you sure you want to do this?" I asked.

"Yes," she said firmly. "It's been my greatest desire to live in the United States."

"Well, I'm happy for you, then," I said, "but I'm also really sad. You're my best friend."

Tina hugged me and promised to write often and send pictures. We were still hugging each other when someone came into the room to announce that there was a man at the door, looking for me. I saw that it was the taxi driver, Antonio. I'd made arrangements to meet him here, but he was too early! I quickly went to greet him, but said I wasn't ready yet. He laughed and said he would wait for me outside.

After saying good-bye to Tina, I went out to meet Antonio, and we decided to go for a walk in the park. We stopped at a store on the way to buy some soda and snacks. At the park we sat on the grass and chatted and flirted with each other.

Antonio reminded me of Tito when he laughed, but Antonio was much older. He told me he was thirty-four years old and lived out of town. He owned the taxi—it was his own business.

I also told him a few things about me, and we had a lot of fun together.

"Can I interest you in dinner tonight?" he asked at the end of the day.

"I'd love to," I answered, "but I can't this time. I have to return to the embassy, because my 'parents' are waiting for me."

He looked puzzled until I explained that the people at the embassy took such care of me, they seemed like my parents. I enjoyed coming home to my "parents;" it really made me feel special that they were waiting for me.

When we got back to the embassy, Antonio said that he wanted to see me again. "I like you very much, Maria," he said. "In fact, I think I'm falling in love with you." He kissed my hand and then said good night. I was very impressed with the way he treated me—he was very caring and a true gentleman.

I wrote back to Tia Trinita the next day, thanking her for her letter and for not forgetting about me. I told her that I had visited Uncle Oliverio, who was well, as were his children and his wife. I told her how happy he was to see me again after so many years. And I asked her if she could tell me when I was born, that I needed my birth certificate. I sent kisses to her, to my aunt Conchita, and to the baby.

The next Sunday, I decided I could not wait any longer to find out my true age. I went to see Uncle Oliverio to ask if he knew when I was born.

"Didn't Tia Trinita say anything to you about your birthday?" he asked.

"No, when she brought me to Father Luna's grange, she forgot to give my information."

He stood up very straight and said, "Maria Luisa, you were born on June 24, 1944."

My mouth dropped open; it was just that simple. "Are you sure?"

He responded, "I'm absolutely sure. I'm as sure of that as I am that my name is Oliverio Morales."

I was happy to hear that. I kept on repeating that date—my birth date!

Then he told me that he remembered the date because my mother had almost died during her labor. He said that I was born on St. Juan's Day, and because of that they almost called me "Juana," but that he had begged my parents to call me Maria Luisa. "I always thought it was a beautiful name," he said.

"Thank God!" I said. "I hate the name Juana!"

I played with the kids for a little while, but it was getting to be late and time for me to go back. As I walked out of the house, my uncle caught my arm and started to cry.

"What is it?" I asked. "What's wrong?"

"I have to tell you something," he cried. "It may come as a shock, but I need to tell you." He took a deep breath and then said, "Maria Luisa, I'm your real father. I had an affair with your mother. I am completely sure that you are my child."

"Uncle Oliverio! I hardly know what to say!"

Natividad was very angry and said that I had put everybody in a great dilemma. "Now my children will have to share their home and their house with you!"

I tried not to laugh. "Don't worry; I don't want to live with you. I don't want anything from you." Then I turned to my uncle. "Don't you worry, either. I will always love you the same, either as a father or as an uncle."

When I returned to the embassy that night, my head was full of many thoughts. I admired my uncle Oliverio, but in a way I wished he hadn't said anything about him being my father. I did not know why he felt the need to confess, but I was very disappointed. I felt that if he really was my father he should have looked for me a long time ago. Had I known he was going to do that, I would never have tried to get in touch with him again. But now it was too late. I thought of how happy I had felt when I first learned that Uncle Oliverio was living in Bogotá, of how lonely I was until I met his family, how pleased I was to feel part of a family again. But now I felt just like before—no, I felt worse. I decided it would be best if I stopped visiting my uncle's house. I would miss his children, but it was too uncomfortable for me to be there now.

There was one thing that made me happy, though, and that was that I finally knew my birth date. I kept on saying the date—June 24, 1944—and I realized that Señorita Anita had been almost right when she'd calculated my age; she was off only by a couple of months. Now I knew how old I was—and the best of all, my birthday was coming up in a couple of weeks! I would be twenty-two years old.

I got letters from my friend Tina; she sent pictures that she took at Cape Cod, Massachusetts. I was amazed by the beauty of the scenery—the ocean, the beaches, the boats. I had never seen a picture of a beach—I grew up seeing only the river. She also said in her letters that there was a big nun's house that she could visit on Sundays. At the nun's house there were some nuns from Spain and Colombia who would rent rooms to young working girls. All of this sounded great, and I was happy for her. In her letter she said that she was very happy, and that moving had been the best decision she had taken in her life. Still, she missed her family and friends and said that she would keep on writing.

Once in a while I would go out with Antonio, usually to the movies. He asked me formally if I wanted to be his girlfriend, and I accepted. He was very sweet, always taking care of me and calling me often.

Eventually the countess asked me about the man who called me so much, so I told her all about him.

"The next time he comes to pick you up," she said, "ask him to come inside so I can talk to him. I want to know what kind of intentions he has for you."

I grinned. It pleased me that she cared so much about me. "I will tell him that," I promised. It was just a week later when Antonio came to pick me up, and I told him that the countess wanted to talk with him.

"Why does she want to talk to me?" he asked. "I can't do that. She's a *countess*!" So we left the embassy without seeing her. Before going to the movies, I wanted to stop at Mother Cecilia's to show her the pictures and the letter from Tina. Antonio waited for me outside.

Mother Cecilia was very happy to see how well Tina looked.

"Yes, she's a lucky girl," I said.

"Would you like to go to the United States?" Mother Cecilia asked.

"Well, yes, but how could I?"

Mother Cecilia smiled. "I know of a place that hires young girls to work in the United States as nannies. The girls I know who are doing this seem very happy at their jobs. And the best thing about it is that after these girls finish with their contracts, they can stay there and work in factories or other places. Why don't you think about it? If you're interested, I'll give you the number of the office to call and apply."

I used to see Mother Cecilia as the light that would show me my way. I was so thankful for her—every day I thanked God for putting her in my path. When I was leaving, I promised her that I would come back soon.

Antonio asked if I wanted to have lunch, and on our way to the restaurant, we passed by the San Diego Church.

"Could we stop here for a moment?" I asked.

Standing in front of the church was Father Luna, holding a piggy bank in his hands, asking for donations for the children in his granges. By now, Father Luna had about a dozen granges in different states throughout Colombia and was well-known throughout the country for his acts of humanity. Part of me wanted to go over to him, to thank him for everything his grange had done for me, for everything that I learned there. But I was embarrassed to approach him because of what he, personally, had done to me. I had forgiven him a long time ago, and had asked God to help him behave, but I still couldn't approach him.

Later, the countess asked me why Antonio had not wanted to talk to her.

"I think he's nervous about talking to a countess," I said.

She said, "That sounds like an excuse, to me. How old is he, anyway?"

"He's thirty-four."

She sniffed. "A man that age probably has a commitment with somebody else. Who knows? He might even have children." When she saw my look of surprise, she added, "The next time he comes for you, ask to meet his family. If he gives another excuse, you should probably leave him alone—he might just be playing with you or looking for a sexual relationship. And if that's the case, he will leave you—if not pregnant, then at least very disappointed."

A few weeks later, when Antonio arrived for our date, I asked him one more time to come inside to talk to the countess.

"Oh, I'll do it when we get back." He looked radiant and happy, so I didn't press him on it. After driving around for a while, he stopped the car and started to kiss me. "I have a marvelous idea," he said. "I have a friend who's away, and he left me the keys to his apartment. Why don't we go there? We can listen to music and be alone. It'll be the perfect atmosphere to talk about all the things that we haven't talked about yet."

The countess's warnings popped immediately into my mind. "First," I said slowly, "I think I'd like to meet you family."

The look on his face turned from jubilant to serious. "But they all live very far away. And they're always very busy."

I thought that maybe the countess was right about him—he only wanted to play with my feelings.

"So what do you say?" he asked. "Shall we go to my friend's place?"

"All right," I agreed, "but first I want to see Mother Cecilia, because Tina sent some pictures for her." Once we got to Mother Cecilia's place, I jumped out of his car and told him that I had changed my mind, that he didn't have to wait for me, because I didn't want to go to his friend's place.

Antonio shrugged. "Okay," he said. And he sped off quickly, without saying good-bye. It was very disappointing, but thank God—and the countess—that I did not fall for his game.

Once inside, I greeted my friends and then told Mother Cecilia that I would like the phone number of the agency. Even if I decided not to do it, it would be good to have the number.

I got another letter from my aunt Trinita; she told me that she was happy I had found my uncle Oliverio. Unfortunately, she couldn't provide my birth certificate. The church that held such certificates had burned to the ground, and all the documents were lost. I was sad about that, but at least I already knew my birth date. My birthday arrived, and my uncle Oliverio called to congratulate me, but I did not tell anybody else; I wanted to celebrate it alone.

Shortly after my birthday, the countess's English bulldog got sick and died. The countess was inconsolable; she'd loved the dog so much. She asked the gardener to make a wooden box, and she asked me to cover the inside of the box with a white cloth. After that, we placed the dog's body inside. Meanwhile, the gardener had dug a hole in the garden. We all stood there together, around the hole, and prayed for the dog. We threw flowers on top of the box, and then the gardener started covering the box with dirt. The countess could not stop crying, and this made me reflect on how a woman could be so merciful and loving toward a dog. It brought home how very different her behavior was from the behavior of the guerrillas who had killed so many people and buried them in public graves without any mercy. This woman's simple action gave me hope: even though I knew that there were cruel people in the world, there were good people, with good hearts, too.

Soon afterward, I decided to call Mr. Ronald's office—this was the place that Mother Cecilia had told me could send girls to the United States. His secretary asked me to stop by his office, and so I left right away for my appointment with him. Mr. Ronald was tall and blond, and of course, he was from the United States.

The first thing that he asked me was who had referred me to his office.

"Mother Cecilia," I said. "I am very interested in moving to the United States to work as a nanny."

He asked me a couple other questions and then said, "You seem to be a good candidate to work in the United States. I'll just need to see your documents—your picture ID and your birth certificate."

When I heard that, I felt defeated.

"Is there a problem?" he asked when I didn't offer any documents.

"Yes," I said quietly. "The church where they were filed burned down. I don't have any legal identification."

He suddenly turned cold. "Well, if you don't have any of those documents with you, why did you waste my precious time?"

"I … I'm sorry," I said. "How can I get my documents?"

He sighed heavily. "Go back to the village where your parents or family members lived and look for the priest of that place. Explain everything about the burned church to him. The priest should know what to do for you."

"Thank you," I said, starting to leave.

He put up his hand. "Wait a minute. You'll need your family members to tell the priest about your birth and the information about your parents. Ask for a letter with a seal from the city hall of that village. That's the first step to obtaining your documents. Once you have that letter, you can go to the city hall of Bogotá with two family members and ask them to sign for you so you can get your first picture ID. Now go at once and do everything I said. Good luck."

Above: This is a picture of me and the countess's bulldog

I left his office thinking about the difficult task I had in front of me. Everything seemed too complicated. I did not want to go back to my village; I was afraid to go back. Even though Tia Trinita told me that everything was safe there, I did not have good memories of that place.

One Sunday I went to visit my friends at Mother Cecilia's place. As soon as I entered the room, one of the girls ran up to me. "I have something juicy to tell you," she said. "It's about that man who used to pick you up sometimes—your boyfriend."

"What is it?" I asked.

She smiled slyly. "He was at the church on Sunday—with his wife and children."

If she had expected to shock me, she was disappointed. Her news did not take me by surprise. I was half expecting something like that—after I'd refused to go to his friend's apartment, he'd never called me again.

16

The countess called all of us for a meeting and told us that she was going to Italy for two months of vacation. She said that we all could take vacations to visit our families, as long as we took turns keeping an eye on the embassy. Everybody was happy, including me. Although I did not plan to visit my family, I was going to have a lot of free time.

Venancio, my new aunt Natividad's son from a previous marriage, had called me one day and asked me why I'd stopped visiting him and the children; he told me that they asked for me and waited for me on Sundays. Venancio invited me to go to the marketplace with him the following Sunday. There was a place there that sold hamburgers and hot dogs, which he loved. We met on Sunday and walked around at the marketplace. We saw beautiful birds in cages—parrots, cockatoos, and many other kinds. I particularly liked one cage, which held several small "fortune-telling" birds: when I put money in the cage, one of the birds picked up a small piece of paper with a prediction on it and gave it to me. It said that I would make a trip far away, sooner then I imagined, and it wished me good luck. Venancio also put some money in the cage to get a fortune—he did it a few times, hoping he would receive the same fortune as me. I bought Venancio a hamburger, and I ate one too, I'd never had one before, and I thought they were so delicious. We spent the whole day at the marketplace.

The following Saturday, I went to the mall to buy the materials to make a dress. I turned—and there in front of me stood my uncle Oliverio. He was coming from work and still wore his policeman's uniform. He was happy and surprised to see me. He gave me a hug and invited me for lunch. As we sat together, we talked about everything we had gone through. I told him about my desire to move to the United States, and how hard it was because I did not have my birth certificate.

"That surprises me, Maria Luisa," he said. "Are you sure that's what you want to do?"

"Yes, it is," I assured him.

"But if you leave, you will be lonely in a strange country. It's really hard to move to another country if you don't know the language."

My answer was quick. "I've been alone all of my life—at least, ever since I can remember. And I can learn a new language little by little."

"I will respect your decision," he said. Then he asked me to buy him a pair of sneakers, a pair of jeans, and a shirt, because he was going to go to Campo Hermoso the following Monday to find my birth certificate or get the sealed letter that I needed from the priest.

I hugged him—I could not believe what he was telling me. "But why are you going to Campo Hermoso?" I asked. "I've never heard of the place."

"Campo Hermoso is where you were born," he explained. "Your grandmother used to live very close to it. It was a village, like Santa Teresa, only further into the woods."

That was another surprise for me, because I always thought I had been born in Santa Teresa. I bought him what he asked for, then I asked him if I could go with him.

"No," he said, "it's a very long trip. First, I must take a bus from Bogotá to a small town called Santa Maria—that will take about five hours. From Santa Maria, I have to ride on horseback for a whole day until I reach Campo Hermoso. I think such a journey would be too hard for you. But don't worry. Once I get to the village, I will look for some witnesses to sign for your parents." He placed his hand over mine. "Trust me, Maria Luisa. I will be back in three or four days."

Oliverio then asked me to call him "Papa," because he believed that he was my father. I felt uncomfortable calling him that, because I had always known him as my uncle, but I thought it was a small price to pay for his making the journey to get my documents so that I could go to the United States.

I went back to the embassy full of joy. I prayed and asked God to give me strength and to give courage to my uncle Oliverio. I trusted him completely.

Just a few days later, Uncle Oliverio called to tell me that he was back, and that everything had gone well. He had that very important paper.

I agreed to meet him at a restaurant the next day. When I saw him, I hugged him with joy.

"Sit down," he said, "you are going to be very happy. Everything went well in the town. I almost missed the priest because he was about to leave for another town—his horses were ready, and he wouldn't be back for two days. So I was lucky to find him."

I was too excited to listen to the story about the priest, and Uncle Oliverio recognized that. He smiled broadly. "Do you remember that I told that you were born on June 24, 1944?"

"Yes, I remember," I said.

"Well, I made you younger by two years! I told the priest that you were born in 1946. Isn't that wonderful?"

I remained silent. Why was that wonderful? I wanted to be older, not younger, but I had to leave the document the way it was.

Then he said, "I wish I could do the same with my birth date and make myself five years younger. Look at it this way, Maria Luisa ... you'll thank me in a few years, when you're twenty-eight instead of thirty. You'll feel younger."

I thanked him for his good intentions, even though it would have been better if he had left the original date, 1944. Once again, I felt like I had no control over my life. Someone else was making the decisions for me.

After lunch, I hugged him and thanked him again for such a big favor. My future depended on it, and everything was going well. I said good-bye, and he walked with me to the bus. On the way back to the embassy, I sat quietly. I had the letter sealed by the priest in my hands—the most desired paper. But it was a lie; my birth date was not correct. Still, Uncle Oliverio had listed Sergio as my father. I knew that could not have been easy for him; he could have just as easily written in his name instead.

The ambassador and the countess left on vacation, and the employees were alone; now I had a lot of free time to begin the process of getting my papers. I followed Mr. Ronald's instructions, and in less than a week I had my papers in order, thanks—surprisingly—to Natividad, who offered to help because all the offices required a witness.

I went to see Mr. Ronald, and he received me very kindly. I gave him all my papers, and he took some photos to send to the family that was going to employ me in the States. "After the family signs the contract," he explained, "you can get your passport and a temporary visa. You'll get the real visa after living in the States for six months."

He said that as soon as he had a family lined up for me, he would call me. The process would take about six months.

At the embassy, I started asking the butler how to say many words in English. I knew some, but I needed to learn more. When the curious butler asked me why I wanted to learn English, I just laughed. I hadn't told anyone about my plans.

Magdalena, my co-worker, invited me to visit her family in the faraway province of Santander. After a tiring six-hour trip by bus, we arrived to find that her parents were not at the bus station. We finally found a hotel room, and immediately went to sleep. I think we had only slept a couple hours when I heard the door open, and someone came into the room. Magdalena started screaming and turned on the light—and we saw an old lady standing there.

"This is my room," she said, "but you can stay here, too. I will sleep in a corner. I just want to make a little money for renting my room."

We calmed down, but I could not sleep. Magdalena, on the other hand, was asleep and snoring the next minute.

In the morning, Magdalena said we had to hurry to the bus stop because her parents would be waiting for us. I was so tired that I looked drunk—I was weaving as I walked. Magdalena thought it was funny, but I was in a bad mood. Then Magdalena saw her parents and hurried toward them. She introduced us, and then we all got on another bus to their house, which took about one hour.

The bus had an opening on the sides and top, and many people carried hens, ducks, and other animals with them; they made a lot of noise. The road was not paved, so the bus kicked up clouds of dust that fell on us. My eyelashes felt hard, and my hair got very dusty and dirty. I looked at Magdalena, and we laughed to see each other's faces covered with sand and dust. It reminded me of when Tia Trinita had taken me to Father Luna's grange—the same thing had happened because the roads were dusty and the truck was open. Now, it seemed funny, especially since the passengers were talking so loudly and carrying smelly animals. I think I had become a little modernized, forgotten my life with my family in Santa Teresa.

We arrived at a house on a hill surrounded by trees and animals, cows, horses, and hens. This was Magdalena's parents' house. I was very tired, so Magdalena took me to a little room where I could get some rest; the bed was made of concrete, but there were some blankets to use as cushions. I rested for a few hours and then got up to find something to drink. Magdalena's mom gave me a special drink called *chicha*, which is made of corn and raw brown sugar put in a big jar to ferment. It had a delicious flavor. I was so thirsty that I had two big glasses, but people can get drunk if they drink too much of it, and I was not used to this kind of drink. I did not feel anything right away, but about ten minutes later I developed an awful stomachache. The pain was terrible. Magdalena's father thought I should go to the hospital, but a neighbor came over and said that she knew how to cure the stomachache. She found three little plain white rocks from outside and boiled them in clean water, then gave me the water to drink. In about three minutes, all the pain was gone. That water was incredible! I asked them not to give me the fermented drink again; I preferred to drink water.

One day we went to a small brook and bathed there, playing in the water. This made me remember those times when I was little and would go with my brothers to play in a brook. We would catch toads and frogs.

As we were going back to the house—we were only about twenty-five feet away from it—the earth started to shake very hard, and we could see the walls of the kitchen tumble down. Thank God, no one was inside. We could hear screams from the neighbors in the distance. We made our way into the house to look for a radio, but the earthquake had caused a power outage. Soon Magdalena's parents arrived and were relieved to see that we were okay. When the power was restored, we heard on the news that this had been a big tremor. Santander had received the worst of it, and as a result there were several casualties.

A few days later, we returned to Bogotá. I thanked Magdalena for taking me with her to meet her family. To my surprise, Elvira told me that Uncle Oliverio had come to visit while I was away. He'd asked that I call him as soon as I got back.

He had big news for me. "Natividad and I are going to visit Aunt Trinita in Santa Teresa," he said, "and we'd like you to come with us."

I was very anxious to see my aunts even though I had very bad memories of that place; I could not forget the things that had happened there. I remained silent.

"The place is much safer now," he insisted. "There shouldn't be any problems."

Finally, I agreed to go with them.

I could not believe I was going back to the place that held such strong and negative memories. Still, I wanted to see Tia Trinita and meet her daughter. I also wanted to see my brothers, or at least hear news of them. My greatest desire was to see my family again.

I met my uncle and Natividad at the bus terminal. Natividad had Patricia, Mauricio, and Nestor, the baby, with her. We bought round-trip tickets, and away we went on our trip to San Luis de Gaseno. I was very surprised to see that the road was paved and well maintained, but after four hours on the road, it became narrow and dangerous. There were huge rocks on the left side of the road, and to the right there was a big cliff with a river at the bottom. A big freight truck went past us very fast and so close that it broke the side mirror of the bus. The pieces of glass flew everywhere, and I realized that I was bleeding from my face—a piece of glass had cut me, but I was so scared that I had not felt any pain. Natividad showed great compassion and took care of my wounds. After a long while we got to San Luis de Gaseno, a little town with about thirty houses. It was Saturday, and there were lots of people around for the market day. I loved this—there were fruits, different kinds of breads, and guava covered with cheese, just like my grandmother used to make for the priest when I was a little girl.

My uncle Oliverio told us that Aunt Trinita would come for us the next day; in the meantime, we would stay in a hotel called Las Brisas (The Breezes). We had a great time that afternoon. There was a river nearby, and we went swimming in water so clear and clean it looked like crystal. We went back to the hotel to get some rest, but it was so hot in the rooms and there were so many mosquitoes that we couldn't sleep. We went to a store and bought some netting to hang around the beds and protect us from the mosquitoes, but that increased the heat and made it hard to get fresh air. When we got up the next morning, we had mosquito bites all over our bodies. My face looked as if I had the measles—the bites, combined with the scratches from the glass, looked quite dramatic. We ate breakfast at a small restaurant in the town, and I noticed that Uncle Oliverio kept looking over at another table. Finally, he got up and walked over, saying in a loud voice, "Is that you, Avelino?"

Yes! I could not believe my eyes! There was my beloved brother Avelino. I recognized him right away, and my eyes got teary as we hugged for a long time. We both were quite moved by this encounter. He told me that Aunt Trinita had told him that I was going to school in Tenza, but that was all he knew about me. We had not seen each other in almost sixteen years, so we had many things to tell each other. He told me that Eliecer had gone to live with my father in a small town not far away, but he had not heard anything from them in a long time. Avelino was working at a big farm, and he had come to town to sell animals. After talking for a long time, I gave him my address and phone number at the embassy. We said good-bye, but we agreed to see each other again as soon as we could. I was so happy to see my older brother again.

Uncle Oliverio suggested walking toward the road, where my aunt was supposed to come for us, and we started off. Finally, we saw her coming toward us with her husband and four horses. My uncle ran to meet them, and we all followed. There was Tia Trinita. Again, my eyes were full of tears. I ran to meet her and gave her a big hug. She was very touched to see me, too. She could not believe how mature I looked; I was a young lady. She introduced us to her husband, who seemed to be very young.

We went back to the little town, because Trinita wanted to buy a few things. She suggested that we stay there one more night and go to Santa Teresa very early the following morning. I agreed, but Natividad and Oliverio decided to return to Bogotá because baby Nestor was sick. I wanted to go back with them, but Tia Trinita insisted that I stay with her; that way, I could also visit my aunt Conchita and the rest of the children.

The next morning we loaded our personal belongings onto one of the horses, and the other three carried Trinita, her husband, and me. When we had been riding for about thirty minutes, my aunt wanted to stop to visit her friend, who used to live in a very poor house. It was a shack, surrounded by a lot of alligators. These alligators were small, only about eight inches long, but they were all over the house. The people who lived there calmly scared them away with a broom so they wouldn't bother us. I had a camera and started to take pictures of the alligators. Everybody laughed about that—because I was taking pictures of the alligators instead of the people.

Once we were back on the road, I thought that my uncle had made a good decision. I could not imagine his children on horses on such a long trail. After a while, I felt like a professional horse rider. We stopped for a little while because I wanted to rest and to go to the bathroom. I had to hide behind a bush to pee, and when I got up, I could not believe what I saw on my legs—they were covered with tiny ants. I screamed very loudly, and my aunt ran over to me.

"Don't slap at them!" she warned me. "Just dust them off carefully, so they don't bite you."

I tried to do as she said, but they bit me anyway. My feet started to swell, and my legs were in pain, as if they were burning.

"You are lucky, Maria Luisa. Sometimes these ants attack all at the same time, leaving lots of poison and causing worse pain."

I didn't feel lucky. I had no medicine with me, and I was concerned about the pain and the infection.

"Don't worry," said Tia Trinita. "Lemon juice cuts any type of infection. As soon as we get to the house, I'll give you some."

We continued our journey. I was very tired, and my legs were killing me. Now it was getting dark, and my aunt suggested that we stay at her friend's house nearby. When we arrived, my aunt helped her friend to make dinner. They made yucca, plantains, and a sauce made out of tomato, cilantro, and onions. There was no meat. The food reminded me of my childhood—my mother and aunts used to prepare the same meal, which had been our favorite.

When it was time to go to sleep, I was sent to the attic and a bed made of sticks covered with hay. I placed my clothes on top of it. My whole body was itchy, and I started to think about ants and alligators. I could not fall asleep, even though I was exhausted.

Finally, in the early hours in the morning, we continued our journey to Aunt Trinita's house. After about an hour, we could see part of Aunt Trinita's house and two people farther up on the hill.

"Those are my children, Gloria and José del Carmen."

I could not see them clearly, but they could tell we were coming, because they were waving white pieces of cloth at us. We started moving faster, because my aunt was delighted to see her children again.

17

It took us a long time to get to the house. It was on a very high hill, and the horses tired easily—so did I. Finally, we came to the house, and the children ran to greet us. I met Gloria, my cousin, and José del Carmen, who had been just a baby when I left. He was a handsome young man, and Gloria was a good-looking girl with long black hair. José del Carmen was sixteen now, and he seemed very intelligent.

Then I saw my aunt Conchita, and I started to cry. She looked very tired; she was losing her hair and her body was very thin. I felt terrible to see her in such a condition. We both ran to hug each other and kept on crying.

"I thought I would never see you again," she cried. "It's a miracle that you're here in front of me." We reached the little house, and once I saw it, I knew that it was not the same house that had belonged to my grandmother. Aunt Trinita said that the old house was on the other side of the hill. If I wanted to, we could see it tomorrow.

Grandmother had given the farm to Aunt Trinita. It was a beautiful place, with gorgeous views in every direction. For this reason, it was also the place where my dad, Uncle Marco, and Desiderio would stand to see if guerrillas were coming from Santa Teresa. All those horrible moments that we had lived sixteen years ago came rushing back, even though my aunts kept telling me that everything was peaceful now.

On the property there was a *trapiche*, which means a spoked wheel in Spanish. The contraption had two very tall spoked wheels that were turned by cows or horses. We would then place the sugarcane in between the two wheels and as the wheels turned it would grind the sugarcane to extract the juice, this juice was later boiled to make brown sugar paste. In addition to the work at the trapiche, there were cows to be herded and milked. Every afternoon, Gloria had the chore of separating the cows from the calves. The calves had to be in a different stable, or they would drink the milk from the cows, and my aunts would not be able to get any milk in the mornings. The cows produced a lot, enough for all of us. But these calves would give Gloria a hard time. It made me laugh to watch her trying to separate them, but I tried to help her. They also had a lot of hens. Some of these hens built their nests in the bushes. They were very sneaky—when we tried to follow them to their nests, they would just walk in circles until we lost them. But if we stayed very quiet, we could track them to their nests full of eggs.

Nothing seemed to have changed in the sixteen years I'd been away. Gloria and José del Carmen did not go to school. When I asked my aunt why they didn't, she said that it was because the school was too far away and it was not safe to send them alone. While we were talking about her children she turned to me and told me that she wanted me to stay with her in the village, and that she really needed my help. I did not know how to respond to her, but I knew that I didn't want to stay. I did not want to hurt Trinita's feelings, so I told her that I would think about it, but I really had no intentions on staying.

Every night while I was there, I woke up to the sound of avocados hitting the ground when they fell from the tall trees. This, too, reminded me of my childhood.

The following Saturday, my aunts and I went to the village of Santa Teresa. The small town had not changed at all—it contained the same small houses and very few people. It was a market day, but there were only about five tables of bread, fruit, and other little things. The people there, though, were extremely nice. They greeted me very sweetly, especially when Aunt Trinita explained that I had returned after being gone for a long time. It seemed to be the same quiet village that I had left. The church was the same, too, and I remembered my grandmother heading there every Sunday with pastries for the priest.

I got tired from walking after a while and sat on a big rock to rest my feet. While I was resting, I saw my aunt running toward me with a stick in her hand. When she reached me, she raised her hand and hit a dog I hadn't seen behind me—he'd been urinating on me! I did not even feel my back getting wet. My aunt hit the dog really hard, because she said that the dog pee was a sign of bad luck—I would never return to that village.

After a week, it was time to go back to Bogotá. Aunt Trinita and her husband loaded the horses, and we said good-bye to my aunt Conchita, who was crying inconsolably, Gloria, and José del Carmen.

Once we were on the road, I remembered something. "We forgot to visit Grandma's old house!" I said.

"Well, it belongs to somebody else now, anyway," Aunt Trinita replied. "I don't like to go there anymore, because even though I have good memories from that house, I also have very bad memories."

"I remember everything about living there," I said. "I guess not all my memories are happy either."

We got to San Luis Gaseno, and the bus was already there waiting for the passengers. As we said good-bye, my aunt gave

me a very strong hug, and it was then that she said she had
something to tell me.

"What is it?" I asked, wondering why she had waited until
this moment to tell me.

"I want you to know that your father asked me many times
to look for you and get you back. He even gave me money for a
trip, but I did not want to do it because I saw that his intentions
were very bad. He wanted you back so you could cook for him
and take care of him. I preferred to have you far away, happy
and getting an education, than living nearby as your father's
slave."

"I've thought about that, too," I told her. "I always thought
that it was better that you took me to Father Luna's grange.
Your decision was the best one."

We hugged each other, and then I got on the bus back to the
capital city of Bogotá.

That bus was totally packed, but I had paid for my ticket in
advance, so I did not have to worry about finding a place to sit.
But about half an hour later, more people got on the bus. One
of them was a lady with a newborn baby in her arms. I offered
her my seat, and she was very thankful for it. I had to stand on
my feet for four and a half hours on that bus.

When I got back to the embassy, the butler was very happy
to see me again. "Now the happiness is back again!" he pro-
claimed. "We all missed you a lot."

That night, as I lay in bed, I realized that I had now fulfilled
my dream of being able to see my family. Although I did not get
to see my younger brother, I knew that he was alive and with
my father. I was happy to be back from my trip to Santa Teresa.
Now I could go to the United States without any guilt.

The following morning, a woman called to speak with me. She was Mr. Ronald's secretary, and she asked me to come to his office—she had good news for me. When I went to his office the following day, Mr. Ronald said that he had found a family who wanted to hire me. "It's a good family," he promised, "and I know that because the wife is my secretary at my office in Boston."

I was thrilled to hear this. He said that this family had two children: one was four, and the other was nine. My job would be to take care of the children, take them to school, and speak lots of Spanish to them. Their mother wanted her children to learn Spanish. She would pay me forty dollars a week. When I heard this, I thought that it was a lot of money. I did not make that much at the embassy, not even in three months. My thought was that I would work in the States for three years, and then come back with lots of money to buy myself a small house. That way, my brothers could come to live with me.

Mr. Ronald told me that I needed to hurry and get my passport and visa as soon as possible, because this lady was in a hurry to have me with them at their house in the United States. He gave me some final instructions, and I left his office. I was very happy with the path my life was taking.

A couple nights later, I was in my room ironing my clothes when the butler came to tell me that there were two men at the door, looking for me. I hurried downstairs—and saw my two brothers, Avelino and Eliecer! I was so happy and excited to see Eliecer. He had been four years old the last time I'd seen him, and now he was twenty. It was a miracle to have both of them there in front of me. We all hugged each other, and between laughs and tears, I introduced them to the butler. Because the ambassadors were still away, I let them both spend the night in my room. Eliecer was a lot darker than Avelino, but very handsome. The following day I took them to the stores and bought many things for them, even watches. I was so happy to have them visiting me. I took them to Uncle Oliverio's house, where Natividad was pleased to have them. I was so thankful to God for that. They stayed there for a week, but before they left, we saw each other one more time. I was absolutely thrilled to have seen them, especially Eliecer. It was a marvelous encounter with my two brothers.

It was time for me to put together my United States wardrobe. I purchased six suits, shoes, and purses that matched the shoes. On the day I received my passport and my visa, I went to Mr. Ronald's office to give him my documents. That same day, he bought my ticket to the United States. The family I was going to work for had paid for half of it, and I paid the other half. My trip was in three weeks.

The ambassador and countess got back from their trip. They seemed happy to be back and had brought us some presents that we liked a lot. The countess had also brought me a couple of satin aprons, one black and one white. They were beautiful; they had ruffles around the edges. She also brought me the black uniform to go with the aprons. I was happy to see them back at the embassy, but I was afraid to tell the countess about my trip to the United States. After several days, I finally summoned the courage, but just when I was going to tell her, she asked me to help her put on her makeup—she had a cocktail party that afternoon. So I decided to wait until the following day to say anything.

That day, I went to the countess's room. I felt that my heart was going to jump out of my chest.

"Come in," she called out when I knocked. She seemed surprised to see me. "What's the matter?"

"Nothing," I said. "That is, everything's fine, but ... I'm going to leave the embassy in two weeks."

"Why, Maria! What's the reason for this?"

I explained to her about my opportunity to work in the United States, but she seemed not to be paying much attention to my story.

"I was planning to bring you to Italy with us in two years," she said, "when we move back." She smiled thinly. "I guess somebody was quicker than I—that person is going to bring you to North America. Congratulations, Maria Luisa." She got up from her chair and went to stand by the window. "I should tell you all the negative things that could happen to you in the United States. But I won't. We don't have time." She whirled around, and it was then that I saw the anger in her eyes. "You need to leave right away. I cannot believe how ungrateful you are! After the way I took care of you! I treated you like a daughter!"

Her words made me cry; I could not hold it any longer.

Immediately, she called the butler and asked him to pay me. Then she turned toward the window again as she gave him a final instruction: "Make sure she's out of the embassy by the end of the day."

My friend Magdalena had known about my plans, so she was not surprised, but the butler and Elvira were in shock. When I had my things collected, I took a taxi to Mother Cecilia's. When she saw me, she laughed. "I see that your desire to leave is so great that you even have your luggage ready."

I explained to her what had happened with the countess.

She smiled. "I knew that the countess would be disappointed by the news. But what is important is that you are happy."

During the week before I left for the States, I visited Uncle Oliverio's children many times. I had learned to love them very much, and I promised them that I would write to them. Uncle Oliverio offered to take me to the airport very early the following morning.

I said good-bye to the nuns, with a special good-bye for Mother Cecilia. Very early in the morning, I got ready and then waited for Uncle Oliverio. He came in a taxi, but as soon as he arrived, he told me not to get in.

"This taxi is noisy," he explained. "I'm going to get you a better one." A few minutes later, another taxi arrived, but it was similar to the first one. My uncle leaned toward the window and shouted at the driver. "Do not think that this young woman, my daughter, is going to get in such an ugly taxi! Go away!"

I laughed at this, but I was also getting nervous because time was passing fast and I had to get to the airport. Finally, a better taxi came along to take us to the airport.

After my documents were checked at the airport, I was sent to the airplane. Because Uncle Oliverio—my father—was wearing his police uniform, he was allowed to go with me onto the plane. There, he took a lot of pictures of me so he could show Natividad that I was really leaving and moving far away. That way, he said, she would stop thinking that they had to share their house with me.

I'd thought that he was taking pictures to keep good memories of me, but he was taking them to keep his wife happy. That was a little disappointing for me, but I was going off to a grand adventure in the United States. I let his actions wash over me and said good-bye with a smile on my face.

PART IV
Coming to America

18

Above: This is a picture of Oliverio escorting me
onto the plane.

Getting on a plane was like a dream to me—it was an extraordi-
nary moment in my life. I was leaving my country and going to
a place very far away, where I did not know anybody except for
Tina or even speak the language. At the same time, I was used
to surprises in my life, such as moving from one place to
another. The only difference was that this time, I had made the
decision myself—and I was conscious of that.

I wanted everything to go as smoothly as possible. Since my uncle had told the priest to write that I was born in 1946, that was the date I was going to adopt from now on. I would write that on every single document I was asked to sign, and I would forget the real date forever. I arrived in the United States on October 7, 1967, and I was twenty-one years of age.

The plane stopped first in Panama; it was very hot. From Panama, we flew to Miami, to Washington, D.C., and finally to my destination: Boston, Massachusetts. It was about eleven at night when I arrived at the airport. A woman was waiting for me—I knew from her pictures that this was Mrs. Judy McCarty. She recognized me, too, and hugged me, welcoming me in Spanish. I said hello to her, very politely. She was a very tall lady with blond hair and blue eyes. She smiled all the time. She took me to her house, which was located in Arlington, Massachusetts. It was a beautiful home, with very fine furniture. The house had four bedrooms and two bathrooms. I had my own bedroom, close to the children's room. The children woke up when they heard us talking. Tom was four and Harry, nine. They seemed to be very sweet. Then I was introduced to Mr. McCarty—Anthony—who was also awake. I knew only a few phrases in English: "good morning," "I am hungry," "thank you," "yes," "okay," and "good-bye." I also knew the numbers from one to ten. That was all I knew, but at least I knew how to say that I was hungry.

That night I fell into bed like a rock. It had been a long day, and I had taken a huge step in my life. Now I was in the United States, and I could hardly believe it. Before my trip, when I would tell people that I was moving to the United States, they would say that I was very fortunate because the country was a world power, and not everybody had the opportunity to come live there.

In the morning, I woke up and got dressed. I was about to leave my room when the children knocked at my door. They wanted to talk to me and get to know me better. We all went downstairs to the kitchen, where they had everything ready for me to make them breakfast—bacon, eggs, toast, and juice. They were happy with me, even though I did not understand anything. They would show me things with their hands, and that was all I needed to understand what they wanted.

After breakfast, they took me by the arm and guided me to their room. Signing with their hands, they showed me that they wanted me to get them dressed and get them ready for school. The contract, I remembered, stated that I was to take them there. Once we left the house, Harry showed me the way. The school was an easy walking distance away, about four blocks away from the house. I was happy and thankful to have been sent to this family.

On the way back home, I stopped to admire some houses. It was October, but I didn't realize at the time that this was why there weren't many flowers, and the plants that were on the ground seemed to be dead. The leaves on the trees were dry and orange. When I went into the house, Mrs. Judy was in the kitchen. She spoke some Spanish, a little twisted, but I was able to understand her. She told me that she was happy to have me in her house, and that the children could not wait to have me there. Then she told me my duties: In the morning, I was to take the children to school. Later on, I was to pick them up and bring them back home. I was to do the laundry, cook, make the beds, and clean and dust the house. The cleaning was easy for me, because I was used to doing that type of job. The only thing

I did not know much about was the cooking. She told me not to worry, because she bought almost everything precooked or frozen. Tom was supposed to be picked up from school at 11:00 and Harry, at 2:30. Mrs. Judy worked at Mr. Ronald's office, and her husband worked in a real estate office.

Mrs. Judy ordered takeout for dinner that night. After that, I gave the children a bath and put them in bed. When I finished that, I had free time for myself.

The following day I called my friend Tina to tell her that I was in Boston. She was very surprised that I was so close to her. She promised to come visit me the following Sunday.

When we saw each other, we hugged and cried with happiness that we were together again. After meeting the whole family, Tina asked Mrs. Judy to let us visit the nuns who lived in Jamaica Plain. She agreed, but told me to pay attention to the bus route and not to get lost. Tina showed me the way so that next time I could go by myself. When we got there, I saw that the nuns lived in two big houses on Pond Street. There were about twenty young girls and six nuns. Tina introduced me to the nuns, who were very nice to me. Most of the girls worked as secretaries, as nannies, or in factories.

The nuns were very young, and they came from different countries—two of them were from Colombia. We stayed there the whole day, and I was pleased to meet these wonderful people. When it was time to leave, the nuns told me that I could consider that my house too, and that I could visit them every Sunday if I wanted a place to watch TV or mingle with other girls.

When I got back, the children and Mrs. Judy were anxiously waiting for me. I gave them the candy that I had bought on my way back, and they took it very gratefully. I was learning some

English, and Mrs. Judy and the children were learning Spanish. It was getting colder outside, so Mrs. Judy bought me a warm coat. It helped me to stay warm. I was not used to this type of cold weather.

In the middle of December, snow started to fall. The children and I went out to play in it. It was amazing; I had never seen such a beautiful thing before. We would spend long hours outside making snow angels and watching it fall. Mr. Anthony would clean the entrance and the driveway with a shovel. I was amazed by the amount of snow Boston received. I had seen it only in pictures, and I could not believe that I was playing with it and enjoying it so much. I felt like a little girl; I have to say that we were like three little kids playing in the snow. Those were wonderful times!

One morning I went out to take out the trash as usual, not realizing that there was ice on the driveway. I fell to the ground, and every time I tried to get up, I slipped again. Finally, I decided to crawl back to the house. Nobody had warned me about learning to walk on black ice, but by falling down and getting up, I learned on my own.

After three months of working for the family, Mrs. Judy had paid me only fifty dollars. I asked her if she could pay me weekly, but she told me that she was saving the money for me. She said that if I needed some money, all I needed to do was ask her.

I bought some records with Colombian music, and there was a record player in my room. During my free time, I would listen to my music, and Tom would run into my room to listen to it, too. He liked my music, and he learned some of the phrases in the songs. He would recite them in a way that made me laugh. He would bring in his records with Christmas songs, and we would have a great time listening to them, these songs I had never heard in my country. We played "Santa Claus Is Coming to Town" and "Rudolph the Red-Nosed Reindeer." Since Harry was older, he preferred to play with his friends. My first Christmas celebration in America seemed very strange to me. The family did not set up a Nativity. Here, they put a Christmas tree in the middle of the living room and decorated it with lights and big colorful balls. And Mrs. Judy wrapped lots of presents for the children. I went to visit the nuns on Christmas night, and they celebrated it a little like we did in Colombia, with a mass to celebrate the birth of baby Jesus.

When I started to get around by myself, I had some difficulties. I wanted to ask people about a lot of things, but I could not. If I was shopping and a cashier told me what something cost, I could not understand how much money I was supposed to pay her. Sometimes people would laugh, and that would embarrass me so much I would leave without buying anything. I soon learned that I loved doughnuts and ginger ale, and I knew how to ask for them. That was all I ate, every time I went out.

At the nuns' I learned that there were records that could teach me how to speak English. I bought one right away, and I started to learn the language. It was wonderful. The record came with a book written in Spanish and English. I could hear a word in English and see it written in Spanish, with its English pronunciation spelled out phonetically. It seemed very clear to me, and that is how I started to speak in English. Listening to these records was my favorite hobby during my free time, so I was learning the language very quickly.

After picking up Tom from the school, we would go to an ice-cream store called Brigham's, which was located about five blocks from the house. We would order our ice cream, and he would tell me about his day. I tried hard to understand him, and we laughed a lot. He was a very sweet and pleasant child. One day he said he wanted to learn to write my name. We were at Brigham's and didn't have any paper, so I grabbed a pen and wrote on a dollar bill: "Maria Morales." I gave him that dollar, and he put it in his pocket.

Once in a while I would ask Mrs. Judy to give me ten dollars. I kept track of it by writing it down, because it was very important for me to know how much money she was saving for me. Tom and I started to take the bus around Watertown to buy candy and window-shop. He was fascinated by our trips.

In the winter, we would make the trip to a nearby hill to go sledding. We would get very wet, but we didn't care because we had so much fun. Spring came, and those plants that had looked so dead when I'd arrived started to bloom again, and the trees grew green leaves. Then it was summer, and Tom and I enjoyed listening to music out in the backyard. He knew some of my songs, and I was able to understand some of his songs, too. He liked to play his Christmas songs, and the neighbors would pass by and laugh at our music. It didn't occur to me back then that the reason they laughed was because we were playing Christmas songs in the middle of the summer.

One day I asked Mrs. Judy for my money because I wanted to open a bank account.

"All right," she said. "I'll write you a check later." But she never did.

I continued visiting the nuns of Jamaica Plain. One Sunday I came back home around 8:00 and passed by the living room to hear Mrs. Judy having an excited conversation on the phone. She was in the library with the doors shut, so she didn't realize that I'd come in. I went upstairs; everything seemed to be very quiet. I entered the bathroom and found Tom sleeping in a bathtub full of water. I woke him up and took him out of the water. He got scared and started to cry. Mrs. Judy came in, and I told her that I had found him sleeping in a tub full of water. She was very thankful for what I had done and, almost in tears, told me that she had forgotten that the child was in the tub.

One day I told one of the nuns that Mrs. Judy did not want to give me my money. She said that if they were not going to pay me, I should leave the house immediately; I should not work for them for free. She also suggested that I could work in a factory, where people made clothes, because she knew they were looking for a seamstress. I'd always loved sewing, and I liked that idea a lot. I went to the factory on a Monday, interviewed, and was hired on the spot. But now I had to decide how I was going to tell Mrs. Judy. And what about the children that I loved so much? Finally, I just told her that I was leaving. And just like the other bosses I'd had in the past, she got very upset with me.

I asked her to give me the money that she was supposedly saving for me, and she told me to come back the following day to pick up a check. I did not have a penny with me, not even for the bus, so she gave me five dollars. The nuns gave me a room with another girl. The room cost twenty dollars a week, including food. That sounded wonderful to me. I was going to start a new job making pants for women at the factory. The following day I went to see Mrs. Judy to get my check. She gave me a check for only $140. She owed me much more than that. It made me sad.

I went to the bank, very disappointed, to open my account. When the teller took my check, she told me that it was no good—Mrs. Judy did not have the money in her account. I started to cry. I could not believe Mrs. Judy had done that to me. She was supposed to pay me forty dollars a week, and she owed me more than a thousand dollars. And now she had given me a worthless check.

I went back to her house to explain what had happened.

"You are a mean person, Maria. You have not thought about everything I've done for you. You are mean, mean, mean! Mean!"

Finally, Mr. Anthony came to the door, and after arguing with him for a while, she told me to get in her car. Mrs. Judy drove to another bank and got me $140 in cash. "Now get out of my car immediately," she ordered. "Good luck." Then she drove off and left me there, alone and crying. I didn't know where to get a bus back to Jamaica Plain. When I finally managed to get back, Tina tried to console me. "I know you'll be okay with the nuns," she assured me. "I'm just sorry for your problems."

Soon, I started my new job. I was very excited. The supervisor gave me some instructions and a couple pairs of pants. I was to sew only the sides of the pants, because the other ladies would do the rest. That was all I needed to do during the whole day. I had some difficulties with the machine at first, because it was industrial and it was very fast. I was afraid to press on the pedal too much. I was used to those old sewing machines at the grange! Most of the other women ignored me—or looked at me and laughed. But there was one woman there from Cuba. She spoke Spanish, and she gave me more instructions. She also told me that the women had treated her the same way when she'd started. "There wasn't anyone here who spoke Spanish," she said. "The rest of the ladies all were Italian."

That day seemed very long, and at the end of my shift, the supervisor gave me some pieces of cloth so I could practice with the machine. In a couple of days, however, I had learned how to use the machine and was able to sew the pants without feeling nervous. At lunchtime the ladies would listen to music. I remember that the song "I Got You, Babe" was popular at the time. Almost everybody joined in and sang along with Sonny and Cher when it came on. That song sounded great to me, even though I didn't understand anything they were singing. It just sounded magical to me.

Working at the factory gave me a lot of free time to talk to my roommates and the rest of the girls. I also spent time writing to my uncle about everything that was happening to me and how happy I was.

After a couple of months, I received a letter from my uncle Oliverio asking me not to write to the house anymore—Natividad did not like it. He gave me a different address to use. This hurt me, because he was the only connection I had with my family in Santa Teresa, and I wanted to know how they were doing. Although everything in this country seemed beautiful and modern, and there seemed to be no poverty, I still missed my family. It saddened me that I had regained them only to lose them again after I left. It seemed that destiny wanted to keep me away from my family.

I did write a letter and send it to the address Oliverio gave me, but I never received an answer. All the letters I sent there came back to me. That is how I lost touch with my uncle Oliverio.

I felt lonely, and I also started to think that if I had a child, I would keep him forever near me; that way, I would never be so alone again. Just the thought of it made me happy, but I did not have a boyfriend—and I didn't see any prospects.

I started going to the Language Institute in the evenings to learn English. I also bought a typewriter to practice typing every day. I became very good at it and was able to type very fast.

After a year of living with the nuns, two other girls and I decided to rent an apartment. We bought some furniture and decorated it very nicely.

Above: A picture of me in my new apartment.

One of the girls met a handsome guy and started dating him. He was well educated and very pleasant. On the weekends, we all went dancing or to the movies. One night when the four of us were out, I met a young man from Cuba. He asked me for a date, and I accepted happily. We went to the movies and to dinner. He seemed pleasant; he was very sweet, and we talked and laughed easily. When he brought me back to the apartment, he pulled me into a dark area and started to caress and kiss me. I responded very warmly. Then he started to kiss my neck in a very hard way, to the point that it hurt me. It felt as if he was peeling my skin off! I stopped that right away, because it did not feel romantic at all. He wanted to come into my apartment—but after that experience, I didn't let him. He left then, feeling really upset. I looked at my neck, and it had lots of bruises all over it. It seemed like I had been bitten by a vampire! My biggest concern was how I would present myself like that at work on Monday.

I was very happy at the factory. We still listened to music on our breaks, and I still enjoyed it. Elvis was a big hit back then, especially his song "Memories." I loved that song. I also loved to watch the *Tom Jones* show on TV. One day I made the other seamstresses laugh because I'd accidentally sewed a pair of pants with very narrow legs, and I said that they were for Tom Jones. They thought that it was funny because he used to wear his pants so tight.

Although things were going well on the job, I decided to look for something else where I could get paid more. That's how I started working at an electronics company, where airplane parts were made. Anderson Power Products was a big company with many departments. It was located in Brighton, Massachusetts.

I liked working there a lot. This company offered great benefits, and the pay was good. One of the first people I met there
was a German woman named Elfrida; she was very nice and
sweet to everybody. I was able to speak more English now, and
little by little, we became friends. I asked her if she knew of a
room or apartment for me. I wanted to move closer to my job at
Anderson. She told me that her neighbor had a room for rent,
and it was only about five minutes from the company.

After work, Elfrida went with me to see her neighbor. She
showed me the room, which cost fifty-five dollars a month. It
seemed very nice, and I decided to move in as soon as possible. I
would be closer to my job, so I would not have to take any more
buses—which meant that I would save both time and money.
After I moved, I was able to spend more free time visiting Elfrida, who was now my neighbor.

Elfrida took me to her house to meet her daughter. It was
snowing a lot, and I was wearing a thick coat and a hat made
out of white fake fur. When we came into the house, I saw a
very pretty girl sitting on the couch. Elfrida introduced her to
me as her daughter, Elvi. She seemed, like her mother, to be
very sweet. She had three small children, and her husband
worked at the police station. Elvi told me that she liked my hat
and smiled. Elfrida's family seemed wonderful to me.

I was very happy to live in the United States, because there
were so many opportunities. I did not hear about many crimes,
and the people seemed to be very nice. I always thought that
moving to Boston had been a good decision.

As time went by, however, my life there did change. My
friend Tina married a Marine and moved to California, and we
eventually lost touch with each other. Also, after I'd lived in my
rented room for a while, the owner of the house started seeing a

man who was almost always there. Suddenly, the house seemed too small for all of us. I decided to move out, which I did, but now I was farther away from my job. That's when I realized that I needed to find a job closer to my new home.

Before too long, I saw an ad for an electronics company that was hiring. It was located very close to my new home, so I called and set up an interview for the following day. When the supervisor saw my application, he said that I could stay and start working that same day. I was excited—I couldn't wait to learn more about electronics.

19

My new apartment cost eighty dollars a month. I soon discovered that after my personal expenses and rent, I could hardly save any money. Then, one day on the bus, I started talking to a girl who worked at the Prudential, the tallest building in Boston. She cleaned offices at night and said that they were hiring people, in case I wanted to work extra hours after my day job. I liked the idea because I could stay busy and also make more money. That was how I ended up having two jobs, one full-time and another part-time. While I was working at the Prudential, I met a girl from Colombia who wanted to introduce me to a Colombian guy she knew, Eduardo Umana. When she described him to me, I realized that he was the same guy who had visited my roommate about a year ago, but by this time they were already broken up. I thought he was very attractive, so I agreed to let her give him my phone number. He called me the following day and invited me to go out with him on the weekend. I accepted without hesitation.

Our romance was over quickly. Even though I had been molested when I was young, I was still a virgin when I started dating Eduardo. I gave myself to him with all my heart, but he said that he was very disappointed by my lack of experience—he did not like virgins. He said that they did not excite him. It broke my heart to hear him say this. I had been waiting for a good, honest man who would love me and enjoy the special bond that comes with physical intimacy, and I chose Eduardo because I thought he felt the same. I was terribly disappointed that I had misjudged him so. From that point on, I began to look at him differently. Little by little, he moved away from me, and I suffered a lot from his coldness. It reached a point where I felt physically sick. I did not want to eat—I would just vomit. Finally, I went to see a doctor, and he told me that I was pregnant.

I was excited by this news, but at the same time I was sad because Eduardo was no longer with me. When I got to my apartment, I knelt down to thank God for the miracle of a baby, a child that I wanted so much. I decided to call Eduardo to give him the news. He told me that he would help me in any way I needed. He promised to call me soon.

Not long after that, I found out that Eduardo was living with a woman who had four children. Eduardo was very happy with the arrangement because the government paid for her apartment, and he could live there for free. Now I knew the reason for his coldness toward me. What an insignificant man he was—and to think I'd thought he was such a wonderful human being. That was the real end of our relationship.

My friends at the electronic company consoled me after they heard of my situation. They told me that the U.S. government had a program called "welfare" that helped single mothers. I applied and was accepted. One of the benefits was that it paid for my visits to the doctor. After the birth, the benefits would help pay my expenses. That made me happy, because it meant I could stay home to take care of my baby until I was ready to go back to work.

I was happy to be pregnant. I bought lots of clothes and toys, as well as a basket for the baby, which I lined with white satin and decorated with lace and ruffles. I went into labor on a Sunday night when the hospital did not have a lot of doctors. There were many women in labor that night, so there wasn't always a nurse or doctor available to help me through the pains. But morning finally came, and it was time to have my baby. It was a difficult birth, and the doctor had to use forceps because the baby was so big—when he was born, he weighed ten pounds. My son was beautiful to me, and all the suffering I went through was worth it because he filled me with so much joy. He was born on December 15, 1970.

Between my weariness and bouts of illness from the labor, I thanked God for sending me my beautiful baby. Elvi came to visit me, bringing me presents and keeping me company. I was so thankful to have her as a friend. Elvi told me that I was like a sister to her, and I felt the same. She asked me to call her in case I needed anything. All of a sudden, although I didn't expect to see him, Eduardo and his uncle arrived at the hospital. I did not have any hard feelings toward him. It was my fault for not getting to know him better before I gave myself to him. He had hurt me, but it did not matter anymore, now that I had this child—my son would never be separated from me. Eduardo begged me to name the child Saul; he said that it was a really nice name and that it was uncommon. "Think about it, Maria," he said. "It could help if he gets lost someday. We'll be able to find him because of his uncommon name."

Finally, I agreed to name the baby Saul Eduardo Morales.

I never saw Eduardo again. I didn't look for him either—I really didn't need him. I had lost the admiration I'd once had for him when I realized how irresponsible he was. It was clear to me that he did not care about his child. I planned to forget about him.

Above: A picture of my first son Saul and I.

I wrote a letter to Oliverio, telling him about my beautiful baby. I wanted to share my happiness with him, but he never wrote back.

As Saul grew, I realized that we needed a bigger apartment, so he could have his own room. I decided to move to Jamaica Plain so I could be closer to the nuns, even though they did not know that I'd had a baby.

When the baby was about six months old, I was standing in line at the post office when a lady touched my shoulder. I recognized her as Catalina; she was always at the nuns'.

"Congratulations!" she said. "I didn't know you had a baby! How do you manage in that small apartment?"

"Oh, I've moved," I said. "My new place has three bedrooms."

Her face brightened. "Really? Would you like to rent one of them out?"

"Well, if it was to a girl, I would think about it, but not to a man."

"I have a guy friend who's looking to share a place," she said. "You should think about making money. Money is all anybody thinks about in this country. You could rent him a room."

Although it was against my better judgment, I ended up agreeing to it.

That same night, Catalina came to my apartment with the young guy. He was very handsome and polite. After looking at the apartment, he asked for my phone number and said he would call later.

He did call me, but not about the apartment—he invited me out. That was the start of a very nice romance. He was very good to me and loved my baby—he was like a father to my son. We would listen to music on the weekends, or he would invite friends over to eat and to talk. Sometimes we would dance. Those were good times.

He did not have documents to work in this country, but he was a mechanic and was making good money. Unfortunately, immigration officials were always looking for people without legal documents and deporting them to their native countries. One day, my neighbor told me that some men had come to her house, looking for people without documents. When my boyfriend heard that, he got very scared. He did not want to go back to Colombia. He liked living in this country a lot better than in Colombia, so he asked me to marry him. If we married, we would be together—and I could give him his residency. We both loved each other and he also loved my son so I agreed to marry him.

That same afternoon, we went to visit some of his friends. When we told them about our plan to get married, they directed us to a church close by their house and told us that the priest was a good friend of their family. We went to see him and ask when he could marry us—and in less than an hour, we were husband and wife. That is how I got married: after only six months of romance, wearing ordinary clothes. I had always dreamed about wearing a white dress and a crown, but it was not meant to be that way. I was a married woman now, and I had taken a very important step in my life.

I think that I was a good wife. I washed and ironed his clothes. I had his meals on time and took care of keeping the house clean. I got pregnant again, and my husband received his legal documents and went to Colombia. He almost missed the birth of his son.

My second son was born on August 14, 1973, and weighed in at about nine pounds. We named him Luis Carlos. I had two sons, and now I did not miss my family in Colombia. My life was full of happiness. It was not easy, especially because I did not have help taking care of the children. My husband worked all day long, and when he got home, he would take a shower and go out with his friends. He had a lot of friends.

Above: A picture of my son Luis.

My friendship with Elfrida and her daughter was very close, and when I had my second child, they came to help me a lot. I was always so thankful for that; they were the only family I had in the United States.

My first child entered kindergarten, and the school was too far away for us to walk there: we either had to take a taxi or wait for my husband. I decided that I needed to learn to drive and buy a car. My first car was not new, but it got me everywhere I needed to go.

Soon, I started going to school to learn keypunch. I paid a lady to take care of my children while I was in school. After learning keypunch, I found a job at the Prudential, the same place where I used to work. I was going to work in the insurance department as a keypunch operator. There were about twenty people working in that department. My desk was really nice; I even got a nameplate. I was proud to see my name on that desk. It was like a dream to be working in the office where I used to clean.

My husband kept traveling to Colombia—and every time he came back, he seemed very different. He began to hit me when we argued. I did not see that as strange: in Colombia, many husbands hit their wives.

On one of his trips, I asked him to look for my uncle; I had forgotten the address where Natividad used to live, and I had lost the letters my uncle had sent me. I wanted to tell him about my children and how happy I was, and I really wanted to know about the family, especially the children. My husband promised me that he would do it. When he came back, I was anxious to find out if he had found them, but he just said that he had forgotten to do it. It was a great disappointment for me. It made me realize that he did not care about my happiness.

One day, when I was at the store where I used to buy doughnuts and coffee as a nanny, I paid the cashier with a five-dollar bill. When he gave me my change, I noticed that the dollar bill he'd handed me had something written on it. It was the same dollar on which I had written my name for Tom, the little boy I used to babysit! I pressed it against my chest and started to cry. That little boy had made me really happy when I needed it the most, when I had just arrived in this country. I used to cry for anything, especially at this moment because it brought back memories. I remember when we used to listen to Christmas music in the middle of the summer in the backyard of his house. I remember how the neighbors would laugh at us because of that, but we didn't care because we loved to play and listen to Christmas music. We really enjoyed those songs; especially "Santa Claus Is Coming to Town" and "Rudolf the Red-Nosed Reindeer."

My husband and I had saved enough money to buy a home, so I begged him to come with me and search for a house one day. He agreed, and we found one in Mission Hill: a three-family house for seven thousand dollars. We went to see it right away, and we liked it a lot. We started the paperwork, and in three weeks we moved in. We took the first floor and rented the other two floors to two families. My son Saul started the first grade, and I enrolled him in a private school. When he put his uniform on, he looked so handsome. For me, he was the most beautiful child in the world. He was very excited to go to school. By now, my children were about the same age as I had been when I saw my mother leave without saying good-bye. I never understood how she could do that, and now, as a mother, it seemed even stranger to me. I would never leave my children, for anything in the world.

After I'd worked at the insurance company for two years, they had to make some budget cuts. There wasn't much work for me to do anymore, so I was one of the employees who had to leave. I was sad to lose my job, but now I could stay at home, taking care of my children. I was happy about that, but now I did not have much money to support them. My husband made good money as a mechanic, but he was a little stingy.

One day after I picked up my children from the school, we went to visit a friend from Colombia. She worked for a company called Blanche P. Field, making custom lampshades from home. We hadn't been there very long when my husband pushed his way into her house, breaking the door. He was angry because I was not home, doing my duties as a housewife. He pushed me out of her house and slapped me on the face as soon as we were outside. He hit me so hard that I almost passed out, and my nose started bleeding. He did this in front of the children, who were scared and crying.

He pushed us into the car and drove away fast. He said he was heading to New York, but I had no idea why he was taking us there. By the time we got to New York, he seemed a lot calmer. He brought us to a friend's house, where we stayed for two days. When we went back home, I called my friend to apologize for what had happened. I still don't know why my husband acted that way.

Once in a while, I would escape to my friend's house and help her with some of the sewing she occasionally did for extra money. She used fine silks and lots of trims, and I really enjoyed it. Everything that had to do with sewing just fascinated me. When she saw how much I liked it, she asked me if I wanted to work with her. It seemed like a good idea, so the next day I went with her to apply for a job.

When we got there, we met with the owner, Warren. He questioned me about my sewing skills, and I told him that I knew how to sew quite well and liked it very much.

Immediately, he sent me to the sewing room. I said good-bye to my friend, and the supervisor gave me a lampshade to sew. When I was halfway done, the owner came to check on my work and told me that I was doing a good job, making very fine and delicate stitches. He said that I was welcome to work at his company. So I ended my day sewing. Then I went back to my house as fast as I could. I didn't know what my future was going to be, but I had a job doing something that I really loved to do—sewing!

That night, I didn't have dinner ready on time. When my husband came home from work and saw that there wasn't food on the table, he got very upset. He didn't even let me explain why I didn't have it ready. He just grabbed a pot that was on top of the stove and slammed it against the floor. He was swearing, and he almost hit me, but he finally just left the house—telling me as he did to clean up the lentils that I had been cooking in the pot, which were now spilled all over the floor. The children were very frightened by the situation, as was I. Incidents like this were occurring more and more often, and getting increasingly violent. It reached a point where I didn't know what to expect, and I often just stayed quiet to prevent an argument.

My mother-in-law, who still lived in Colombia, came to visit us at around this time. She was a very sweet and elegant woman. While she was here, my husband treated me very well. We took her several different places, and she was very pleased with her visit to the United States.

One day she asked me about my family, and I mentioned that I wanted to see my uncle again—it had been a very long time since I had heard from him or my family. She said that as soon as she went back to Colombia, she would try to help me find him.

It was only about a month after she went back to Colombia that I received a letter from my uncle Oliverio. My mother-in-law had used a radio station called Santa Fe to find him, mentioning his name on the air and asking for information about him. He sent me the address where he was living with Natividad and the kids. He also sent pictures of the kids and congratulated me on my two boys—my mother-in-law had shown him pictures of them. I was happy, and very grateful to my husband's mother for the great favor she had done me.

20

Not long after his mother returned home, my husband took another trip to Colombia and was gone for a couple of months. During that time, one of my friends invited me to a party. There was a band providing live music, and soon a very handsome young man came over and invited me to dance with him. I accepted his invitation gladly. We danced all night long. When the party was over, he begged me to give him my phone number; I did, but I didn't think he'd actually call me. But as I was walking into my house after the party, my phone was ringing. We talked a lot that night, and he called me every single day—sometimes four times a day. He was so persistent that I agreed to go out dancing again with him and my friend. That night we danced until very late, and then he invited us to dinner. While we were sitting in the restaurant, he started to kiss me, right in front of my friend.

"Do I have to remind you that I'm married?" I teased.

"Your husband isn't here," he answered. "And maybe he's in Colombia doing the same thing."

After dinner, he followed us to my friend's house. I told him that he couldn't follow me to my house because if the babysitter or a neighbor noticed anything, they would tell my husband when he'd came back. I didn't want any trouble with my husband, especially now that he hit me for any little thing.

This guy—José—kept calling me every day, and I have to admit that I loved all the nice words he used with me. We would often talk almost until midnight. One day he invited me to dinner, and afterward he took me to his apartment. This was the first time we'd ever been alone together—we always went out with my friend. Once we were there, he told me how much he loved me; he said he was going to fight for me. And between all the caresses and his sweet words, I couldn't resist: we made love. I wasn't thinking about any consequences at that time; I just responded to his affection. José told me to get a divorce.

I looked directly into his eyes. "It's not as easy as it seems. My husband is a very violent man. I'm afraid of what he might do."

Eventually, though, his persistence was so great that I filed the divorce papers. I knew that I was falling in love with him, too.

Meanwhile, it was almost time for my husband to come home from Colombia. All this time, in his absence, he had never called me or written me a letter. I wasn't even sure when he would return, until he showed up one afternoon with his luggage. We exchanged a cold greeting, but the children were excited to see him back. I called José right away and told him about my husband's return.

He was silent for a moment, and then he said, "Tell him that you've filed for divorce. I'm going to look for an apartment for us and the kids."

"Take it easy," I urged him. "I told you it's not as easy as it seems to you."

Now that my husband was home, I was living a double life. My husband was always working; he came home only for dinner, then he went out with his friends. After he did, I would sneak out and spend time with José.

One day, Saul fell and hurt himself. Every time the kids fell, my husband hit them just because he didn't want to hear them cry. That's what he did that day; he started to hit my son. That was the last straw for me. I looked at him sternly and said, "That was the last time you will ever hit him. I've filed divorce papers. I don't want to live with you anymore."

He did not even look at me. "You can do anything you want," he said. "I don't care." And then he left. He came back the next morning.

When he received the divorce papers, however, he said he was not going to sign anything. By this time, José too was angry—because I hadn't yet agreed to move in with him. I decided what I really needed was to get away from both of these men and start a new life with my children. Even though I loved José, I did not want to be with him now.

Soon afterward, my sons and I moved to a new apartment. José was excited that I'd moved away from my husband, but I told him that I wanted to be alone for a little while. He accepted that, and said that I could count on him for anything.

I was at the market, a couple of days after I moved out of my husband's house, when I saw that he was following me. He approached me and asked me, very calmly, why I had moved out. He walked with me out of the market and into the parking lot, where he convinced me to get into his car. He drove us to my apartment.

There, he promised me to change his behavior toward me. When he left, I called José, who told me that I needed to choose between the two of them. My husband came back to my apartment that evening, and it seemed that he had no intentions of leaving; he ended up spending the night. Later, I saw José's car parked out front and realized that he knew that my husband had been there with me all night.

It seemed that moving had not helped me at all. Actually, it was more stressful because José felt free to follow me, and my husband dropped in whenever he felt like it. I was nervous and did not know what to do.

I talked to my lawyer, and he told me that the divorce would be final very soon, that my husband did not have to sign any papers for that to happen. José kept calling me at my house and at my job. He was waiting for me outside my workplace one day, and I could not resist his words; I still loved him, and I went with him to his apartment. Once there, we shared our love one more time. We cried at how difficult it was for us.

Trying to decide between these two men was hard for me—especially since what I really wanted was to be on my own. I remembered how lonely I used to be and reflected that now, with two children and two men who wanted to be with me, I missed my freedom. It made me think that life is full of surprises. I also thought that maybe my mother had had a similar problem. I was beginning to understand her a little bit—but I could never leave my children, and I would never understand how she had.

My lawyer called me a few days later, and I went to the courthouse to get my divorce. After answering the questions the judge asked me, I was granted the divorce. I called José as soon as I could to give him the news. He congratulated me for taking such a great step in my life. Within a few days, José called me at work; he had an apartment all furnished, in a city called Chelsea. I began by moving bags full of my children's clothes and belongings to the new apartment. I left the heavy things for last. José had already moved in and was very helpful during my move.

Finally, I took the furniture that I had bought myself. Then I wrote a letter to my ex-husband, in which I explained that our separation was for the best. I asked him not to worry about the children. And I told him not to look for me because I would never return to him.

Two weeks went by, and I was very happy in my new home. But when the doorbell rang one afternoon and I looked out the window, I got a scare. It was my ex-husband.

"What do you want?" I called out to him.

"I don't care what you do with your life," he barked at me, "but please let me see the children."

"No! Go away!"

He insisted, however, and I ended up sending the children out to him. He hugged them and was very happy to see them. The children were happy as well. Later, he told me that he would come to pick them up on the weekend; he said good-bye to the children and left. José and I hugged happily because our worst fear had just been realized, and now we could live in peace. José had a seven-year-old son from a previous marriage. He was named José, as well, and came over often to visit and to play with my boys.

Now I could start my life over with José and my children.

José brought me to meet his family; he had been born in Puerto Rico, but almost all his family was here in Boston. They were a big family, and they all made me feel welcome, especially his mother. She was a very loving and pleasant lady. We continued to live our lives happily; I worked at the lampshade company, José worked at a curtain factory, and my children went to school.

After six months of living together, José asked me to go with him to visit one of his sisters, who lived in New York. It was the night before Christmas, and his sister gave us a warm welcome. She appeared to be a wonderful lady. She had three beautiful daughters. After dinner, I felt dizzy and wanted to vomit. José was worried when he saw me sick, but when I told him that I might be pregnant, he began to jump for joy. He said that this was the most beautiful Christmas of his life.

When we returned to Boston, I went to see the doctor and he confirmed that I was pregnant. I worked until I was eight months into the pregnancy, and I felt well the whole time. The delivery was very complicated, though, because the baby was very large. Ultimately, I needed a caesarian. My daughter was a big, gorgeous baby; she weighed ten pounds. José did not leave me or the baby for a minute. During my time in the hospital, he slept on the floor in my room; he never separated from us. Meanwhile, my children were with Elvi. She was my closest friend, closer than my own sister could have been. I was glad the children were with her.

My daughter was born on September 1, 1979, and I was delighted that my beautiful little girl had finally arrived. It had been my dream to have a girl, and we named her Melissa. Some of José's family came to visit us, including his mother. She was glad to see how happy José was, especially with his daughter. I had no doubt in my mind that José was a good man; he shared everything with me, and I was very happy to have found him. We decided, however, that we were happy not being married for now.

The lampshade company sent me work at home so that I could take care of the baby and my other children, and I was very grateful for that. By the time Melissa was three years old, we had managed to save enough money to buy a house. José made small repairs to bring the house up-to-date, and I decorated it, kept it clean, and organized it.

One day I got a call from my supervisor at work; she said that she was retiring and asked if I was interested in taking her position at work. She said that in her opinion, I was the most qualified for the job. Together, José and I decided that I should take the position. With my new job, I would have a lot more responsibilities.

Many years went by. We decided to sell the house and buy a bigger one, with more room for the children to play. Our new house was in Malden. It was a two-family house with a huge patio, and the children all had their own rooms.

We were living like any other couple with children in the United States; everything was pretty normal. I thanked God for giving me the idea to move to this country. My life in Colombia would have been different. I might still have been working as a housekeeper, without the opportunity to have a family or be a homeowner. But now I was the mother of three children, and I had a good-paying job with benefits. There were times when I would remember how poor I had been as a child. But today, thanks to God, my children had everything—they were going to school and enjoying a comfortable life in the United States. At the age of ten, my son Saul was already working, delivering newspapers. He liked to keep himself busy. By the time he was fourteen, he'd found a job at a restaurant. At the end of his first week, he received his first paycheck, which he gave me so I could buy things that we needed in the house. He was a marvelous child, who gave me constant joy.

Above: This is my daughter Melissa.

I invited my uncle Oliverio to visit me in 1986, and he was very pleased to do so: it was like a dream come true for him. He had always wanted to come to this beautiful country, and now he had that opportunity. I took him many places. We went to New York to see the Statue of Liberty and the Twin Towers. We took lots of pictures. The children and I spent unforgettable moments with him, and he really enjoyed his stay with us. But it was during his visit that he had to give me some sad news from home—my aunt Trinita had died. He had not wanted to write it in a letter; he had wanted to tell me personally. I was devastated by this news. She had been such a special person in my life. I had always loved her, even when she lived far away from me. I always kept her memory close to me, so it felt as if I had lost a part of my life. A month later, Oliverio went back to Colombia, taking back lots of wonderful memories of his time in Boston.

José wanted to earn some extra cash, so he found a second job that was only a couple of hours each night. The money was good, and he enjoyed the work. In May of 1988, José went to work just like any other day—except that on this day, he did not come back at his regular time. The night went by, and I was very distraught because he never stayed out so late. I decided to call the police, but there had been no accidents reported. By the time the sun came up, I had not slept and still did not know where José was. Finally, I got a call saying he was at Mass General Hospital—there had been a car accident.

I rushed to him. He was in intensive care after having had brain surgery, and he was now in a coma. I cried inconsolably.

When the police gave their report, I learned that José had run a stop sign and was hit by a taxi. The impact was so strong that

José was thrown out of his car—about seventeen feet—and landed when he hit a wall.

Above: A picture taken during Uncle Oliverio's
visit to Boston, Jose is to my right.

Days went by, and I wondered if he would ever come out of his coma. Then, finally, I heard him say that he was cold. I was so excited to hear him talk! But there were no more words after that, and he deteriorated with every day that passed. He suffered a stroke and stayed in intensive care for two more months. His family, his mother, and I suffered together. But we still had a small seed of hope that he was going to get better. Then, after he had been in the hospital for three months, the doctors and nurses called me to a meeting. They said that José would never be able to speak again, that he was paralyzed from his hips to his feet, and that he needed to be transferred to a rehabilitation facility.

I had wanted to believe that things were going to be the same as before, but I knew now that everything would be very different. José had to have surgery on his throat and stomach; doctors needed to create an opening so he could breathe and be fed liquids. It was really sad to see him like that; he had been a very strong and healthy man.

While José was in the hospital, my life got pretty complex. I was asking for too many days off, I had too many bills to pay, and now I had to do it alone. I did not have José's help anymore.

I spoke with a hospital-provided social worker, who said that I needed to take care of my children, because José was going to stay at the rehabilitation center; he was in a vegetative stage and he would not come out of it.

I could not believe what was happening. How was I going to cope on my own? Years went by, seemingly in an instant, and it was time for Melissa to have her first communion. It was a very important event in her life. So I started teaching her the prayers and catechism. That way she would be well prepared to receive her communion. Six months before her communion I started to make Melissa's dress; I wanted it to be special. The dress had long sleeves made of lace with sewn-in sequins and pearls, it had puffy lace at the shoulder, and then the sleeves were tight. The bodice was made of white satin, lace, and pearls; it also had a lace ruffle along the collar. The skirt was made of white chiffon and lace ruffles, ruffles were everywhere. The skirt was very full; there was one ruffle on top of the other.

Above: My daughter on her communion day wearing the
dress I made for her.

My older son had graduated from high school; he was working and had saved some money. For Mother's Day that year, he had bought me a dog, a Chihuahua. That little dog was a joy for me and my kids—we named him Chico. Saul was a popular guy—especially among the girls, who seemed to follow him everywhere. He started dating a girl he had met at school around that time, and they seemed to be happy together. Nine months later, she gave birth to a precious child. They named him Saul Jr., making me a grandmother for the very first time. He was born in November 1990.

José's condition remained the same. I was working hard to sustain the family and the house. Thanks to God, the money I was making was enough to save a little.

When my first grandchild was two years of age, Saul and his girlfriend had a set of twins. They were named Michael and Nicholas, and they were beautiful. My family was growing, and I was happy. I had three children and three grandchildren. What else could I ask for? I was very satisfied with my achievements and with my family here in the United States.

Luis, my younger son, was doing well in school. He liked to wear nice clothes: he was named "Best Dressed" in his yearbook. He graduated from high school and went to U-Mass Boston to study biology and medical technology. Saul decided to visit Colombia to meet the family members we had there. He stayed there for almost a month and was amazed by the natural beauty and by the culture he learned about in the museums. He was very well treated there, especially by my uncle Oliverio. He came home with wonderful stories about the country.

Above: A picture of my uncle Oliverio and
my aunt Conchita, she died not too long after Oliverio.
Unfortunately I never had a picture of my aunt Trinita to
show.

Melissa's fifteenth birthday was around the corner. This was
an occasion to celebrate—the time when families introduced
their daughters into society; the time when a girl became a
young woman. For her special birthday present, Melissa chose a
trip to Europe. It was decided that she and I would go with
José's sister and her daughter, who was of the same age. First,
we visited Spain, and we were delighted to see such a beautiful
place. We visited the Royal Palace in Madrid, as well as towns
like Toledo and Seville. We went to Paris next, where we visited
all the tourist sites—the museums, the Arc de Triomphe—as
well as some of the natural wonders. We stood along the Seine,
which seemed full of boats and was just beautiful. Looking up at

the Eiffel Tower, I remembered a time long ago when I'd seen the president of France as he rode past the embassy. Back then, I could not have imagined that I would ever visit his home country. I realized that I had come a long, long way.

When we returned from our trip, I went back to work and the kids resumed their normal lives. A couple years after our trip to Europe, in 1996, I received a call from Colombia—my uncle Oliverio had died from a heart attack.

Once again, I felt my heart breaking. I made up my mind to go to the funeral, and I bought a ticket to Colombia the next morning.

Once in Bogotá, I was greeted by Uncle Oliverio's children, my half siblings. They had been very little when I left for the United States. They were married now, with children of their own. It was hard to believe that I had not seen them for twenty-nine years. At the cemetery, we all cried—except Natividad. I did not see her crying at all. It seemed that her heart was like a stone. I wanted to visit the rest of the family in Santa Teresa, but my cousins were not in the mood to go with me, and I did not want to go by myself: I remembered how arduous the trip was, from the last time I'd attempted it.

At least it seemed that my cousins were doing well; they all had their families and jobs. That made me happy. I had to return to my home, but I promised to visit them again soon.

A few days after I got home, I received a call from my brother Mauricio—whether Oliverio was my father or my uncle, I called his kids my brothers and sisters. He called to tell me that he and his siblings had visited the rest of the family in Santa Teresa, and that the road there, while still full of rocks and hills, was accessible to cars. He had information about the family as well. José del Carmen, now about forty-five years old, was doing well. To me, he was still the baby I had left behind when I was seven years old. After a long conversation, José del Carmen had told them that my cousin Desiderio had died of a heart attack.

I was touched by everything Mauricio told me. And I was pleased to learn that Mauricio and his siblings were able to meet José del Carmen. But the best news came at the end of the phone call. José del Carmen had located my brother Avelino. My heart soared at this news. After losing so many important people in my life, I was thrilled to be able to reconnect with my brother. He had a phone number, and I was able to reach him a short time later.

I was very happy to hear my brother's voice. We talked for a long time, and he told me that he never married or had children. Unfortunately, he did not know anything about Eliecer.

I filled him in on my life, and he was happy to know that I was doing well. That day I was thrilled: I was talking with my "soul brother" after thirty years of not communicating with him.

Mauricio, his wife, and his children eventually came to visit me, and I was very happy to have them here and show them the sights. They now come to Boston every five years.

I am still working at Blanche P. Field, which is located at the Boston Design Center. I have been with this company for thirty years now, and I plan to retire here. Blanche P. Field's customers include famous design companies such as William Hodgins, Bierly-Drake and Frank Roop, and famous people such as John Travolta, Martha Stewart, and Bill Gates. Martha Stewart was so interested in our lampshade techniques that she sent her film crew to our showroom for a segment on our lampshades. Other people, such as the Keno brothers from *Antiques Roadshow*, have also come to film. Even *The Boston Globe* and *The Herald* have come a few times to put us in their home section. Sewing, to me, has been a form of art, and to be able to create beautiful, handmade lampshades is wonderful to me. I am proud to have contributed to this prestigious company.

I am also proud to say that all my children were born in America, and that they are all happily living their lives here. My son Saul has his own construction company and is no longer with his first girlfriend. He has married and is father to another beautiful boy named Sebastian, who is now ten months old. My other three grandchildren are now teenagers and are doing well. Luis moved to California, where he works as a mortgage broker; he currently has no children. My daughter Melissa completed her bachelor's degree in Psychology and is currently finishing up her nursing degree; she also has no children at this time. José currently lives in a nursing home in Cambridge. He recognizes family and communicates by motioning and nodding his head. We visit him often. God has taken me on an unforgettable journey, and I am glad my life turned out the way it has. I came by myself to a new world, not knowing its language, and have created a life for myself and a growing family. I still own the house in Malden that I bought with José, and I have bought a second home.

My life has been full of happiness, despite the heartache I've endured. I have told my daughter Melissa about some of the things I went through during my childhood: I have told her about the times I was hungry and would look for sweet potatoes in the fields, or when the train almost killed the girls from the grange. My stories are hard for her to comprehend—none of my children really understand what it is like to live in a Third World country.

Some years, for my birthday, my daughter would give me a blank diary and ask me to write down all the little stories I would tell, so that one day we could put them all together to make a memoir. I would just look at her and smile, and I would put the diary away. I couldn't tell her that I didn't want to remember my childhood in Colombia. I just said that I was too busy—eventually, I had a collection of blank diaries and notebooks, but I was not interested in writing anything.

But as the years went by, I realized that my life is the legacy I will leave to my children. I also realized that I should fill those diaries with the moments of my life, for my children, my grandchildren, and my grandchildren's children. I see now that it's important for them to know about that little girl from the village in Colombia, who lived much of her life at Father Luna's grange, and who came such a long way from her humble and modest beginnings.

I am truly a fortunate and blessed woman. I thank God for helping me to move forward on my own.

Clockwise from center:
Sebastian on my lap, Nick, Saul Jr., Melissa, Saul, Gisselle,
Luis and Mike.

978-0-595-44280-
0-595-44280-3

Printed in the United States
201282BV00002B/79-96/P

9 780595 442805